Using Computer Games Across the Curriculum

Using Computer Games Across the Curriculum

First published 2012 by
Bloomsbury Education
An imprint of Bloomsbury Publishing Plc
50 Bedford Square, London,
WC1B 3DP

www.bloomsbury.com

ISBN 978 1 4411 0829 6

A CIP record for this publication is available from the British Library.

Typeset by Fakenham Prepress Solutions, Fakenham, Norfolk NR21 8NN
Printed and bound by CPI Group (UK) Ltd, Croydon, CR0 4YY

1 3 5 7 9 10 8 6 4 2

To see our full range of titles visit www.bloomsbury.com
For more information and suggestions from Karen Anderson visit www.karen-anderson.org

Contents

Introduction

Using This Book

This book is designed to be used within any subject, with any pupil of any age group. Although the activities have been created with 11+ and 16+ in mind, they are – in the main – adaptable for younger or older pupils. Throughout the book there are suggestions for subjects or areas where each activity might best be used, but please feel free to adapt the activities to suit your own subject and teaching style. I hope this book becomes a launch pad for new and exciting ideas for your lessons and activities.

Whether you choose to read this book in order or dip into it for reference when needed, I hope that it is enjoyable and useful to you and to your pupils.

Each activity is clearly highlighted and includes:

- the equipment needed (if any)
- the length of preparation or setup
- the suitability of the activity e.g. starter, plenary
- a detailed description of exactly how the activity should be run
- any possible extensions or alternatives

The activities are listed in the Contents at the beginning of this book. However, there is also a Subject Matrix and Skills Matrix (pages 92 and 96) if you need a quick reference. Words in **bold** are included in the Glossary at the back of the book on page 88 and all games mentioned in the book are listed in the Index of Games at the end of the book.

In every school there is always at least one pupil with a reputation for being the 'naughty kid'. They will be talked about by the staff and every teacher in the school will know their name. One fraught-looking teacher may enter the staffroom and say, 'I've just had "naughty kid" ...' and all the other teachers will nod and mutter in understanding. You may never have taught them, you may never have even seen them, but the mention of their name will make your blood run cold and you will automatically be on your guard if they turn up in your class. Computer games have a similar reputation, especially in the world of education.

Teachers are increasingly enthusiastic and confident about using ICT in teaching and schools are increasingly supportive; but there is this 'naughty child' sat in the corner and that's computer games. They are a huge part of the IT industry and yet education is very wary of them, not sure what to do with them.

Often the only time many teachers will have heard about games will have been in a negative sense. Perhaps it was a news story about a computer game that purportedly makes teenagers more violent, or maybe an anecdote about a child who has been playing them too much and as a consequence is now struggling with their studies.

However, just like the 'naughty kid' in your classroom, you should give computer games a chance. They are very often misunderstood and suffer from prejudgement. I have never yet met a teacher who has introduced computer games into their teaching and regretted it. This book aims to give you the support, knowledge and ideas to add these games to your teaching toolbox.

If you have a positive view of computer games, perhaps from playing them yourself or even already using them in your teaching, then this book aims to stimulate your ideas further and suggest new and innovative ways of integrating them into your lessons and activities.

I am not suggesting that you should use games in every lesson – quite the opposite, in fact. One of the benefits of using computer games is that it is special, different and unusual and your pupils will respond to this. If you use them all the time, as with any other teaching technique, games will become staid and lose their magic.

Additionally, I do not propose that you rush out and buy the latest games **consoles** for your school, nor present your accounts department with a hefty bill for new technology. Many of the suggestions in this book are free, low cost or can use the equipment you already have in school. Although using computer games does have the propensity to be pricey, it is not necessary to have the latest whizz-bang technology and it can often be more effective if you do not. And remember that troublesome child I mentioned? Using games in your teaching might be a way to encourage them as well!

Why Use Computer Games?

Computer games can be seen as trivial and inconsequential; how can they help us educate and inform young people? There are several aspects to games that can provide us with exciting teaching and learning opportunities:

- Fun – by being inherently designed to be enjoyable, games can provide some light relief, make a dull topic more interesting and provide a different approach.
- Engaging – games can draw in pupils who may lack confidence or be disinterested in learning.
- Practical – although some games rely on audio or visual skills, they are generally very kinaesthetic, in a way that other learning methods often cannot match.
- Inclusive – for pupils that are weaker, those with special educational needs or gifted and talented, games can provide a platform where all can be involved and the playing field is levelled.

- Competition – the spirit of positive competition is an important attitude to learn during childhood, and games provide a safe environment in which to do this; it also gives children the opportunity to learn to be a 'good loser'.
- Skills development – games will often develop skills such as literacy, numeracy, logic, coordination, communication, teamwork and many others, without those playing even being aware that they are engaging in skill-building.
- Learning without realizing – when playing games it is possible to gain a great deal of knowledge without realizing any learning is actually taking place.
- Rewards – winning a game, whatever it may be, can be rewarding and give that pupil a sense of achievement and accomplishment – and using games as the reward itself can be a good motivating tool, too!

New Ways to Deliver Lessons

Computer games are a powerful tool that can instantly get the pupils' attention and make less interesting subjects more exciting. They can also offer a different method of delivery. Games can be prepared for a particular slot in your scheme of work or they could be introduced instantly when needed. You may keep one in mind when working on a particular topic and, if you feel the pupils need a different approach or a bit more 'zing' in the lesson, you could drop it in, as though you meant to all along.

Setting the scene

By using them to highlight a point or underpin a theory, computer games can provide a vehicle to a deeper understanding. For example, when studying World War II in History, if the pupils play the early *Call of Duty* games (2003-2006) they will gain a powerful understanding of the realities of war as they are not just watching but are immersed in a very authentic, very accurate interpretation (see page 43 for more details).

Games are fun – discuss

Games can be used to start debates and discussions (see section 5 on page 77). They can be effective in many subject areas, but especially so in PSHE, Citizenship, General Studies and other analyses of society and culture. Games provide a shared frame of reference for pupils, so they can debate issues with more coherent arguments based on a common ground. Suggested topics could include gender, religion, race, science and violence. By starting a discussion with a picture of Pikachu from *Pokémon* or a gangster from *Grand Theft Auto*, depending on the age range, pupils will generally find these images provoking and may already have opinions and have heard stories in the media.

Making it up

Another way to use computer games is to have the pupils create their own, targeting the areas of learning relative to the subject material. It could even be an opportunity for cross-curricular learning. You may be concerned that using computer games in class might be difficult to manage, require a lot of equipment or take a lot of preparation or setup. However, in reality it is usually very straightforward and this book will give you guidance and the confidence to try it out.

Children's Development

Solving puzzles

On an individual level, computer games encourage development in players of all ages, from young children to adults. They exercise the brain, just like a crossword does. This is most evident in games like *Dr Kawashima's Brain Training* (on Nintendo DS) but even *Lara Croft*, whatever criticisms there are of her, has to solve puzzles as she jumps around in those short shorts.

As children are developing, one of the first innate tasks they perform is pattern recognition: identifying faces is key to know who is safe and who will look after them. From that point all recognition uses the same process, for recognizing a table, a sunset or a seven-letter word in Scrabble. Playing games can help develop those skills; for example, *Tetris* and its set of seven falling **tetrominoes** are repeating patterns that we learn and, as we become more familiar with them, we can place them in lines faster.

Improving dexterity

Games can improve dexterity. Gamers' hands know instinctively where the *i* key is on the keyboard to bring up their inventory, or console players might know where the *X* button is to cast a spell. The Nintendo Wii, a revolutionary console released in 2006, took this to a new level, with a wireless **controller** that can detect motion and rotation in three dimensions – in other words, more physical interaction and movement is required. For example, when playing tennis the controller becomes a racket and you move as if you are actually playing.

In 2010 Microsoft went one better and introduced Kinect. This is also a motion detection device but does not involve any controller. The player just stands in front of the sensor and Kinect can detect whole body movements, and also some voice commands. Being a relatively new piece of technology, there is more and more being added to Kinect as developers find innovative ways of using its functionality. Both of these products promote the idea that playing computer games can mean moving around, being healthy and playing with others.

Social interaction

Competition and challenge are two features that can keep a gamer playing, whether it is against the computer or real people. Modern gaming has opened up a whole new world in terms of social interaction. What was once a very solitary experience, gaming can now be performed in a global arena from the comfort of your own home. This can be done through a PC (for example, on **MMOs – Massively Multiplayer Online** games) and on consoles (using Xbox Live, Wii Online and PlayStation Home). One person sitting in their living room can now play with people from all over the world and communicate with them through headsets with speakers and microphones. There are, of course, eSafety concerns about this, which are addressed on page 19.

Real world simulation

Games can provide practice for the real world by simulation. The boom in sales of skateboards after the release of each instalment of the Tony Hawks' skateboarding games shows that games encourage children (and some adults) to try an activity or sport for real. *Guitar Hero* and *Rock Band* have done the same for musical instruments. However, games also give you the chance to try these things without the risks of the real world. If you fall off your skateboard in Tony Hawks, you do not really get injured, but your character does. This demonstrates that actions do have consequences: a lesson that can be learnt effectively without having to break your own bones.

Finally, games are important because they are part of modern culture; they are a large part of the lives of the pupils you teach. Just like film, television, advertising and even spoken and written language, games are here: they are integrated in society and they are here to stay.

What Are Computer Games?

Games are everywhere. They are part of everyone's daily life, even though you may not realize it.

From the beginning of a child's life, games are a significant part of interaction with others, such as playing peek-a-boo. As children get older, they learn to play with other children. Games in the school playground, in the park with friends or in the house with siblings can be not just fun but also the opportunity to get exercise, develop the skills of socializing and communicating and also learn values such as fairness and including others. Children may also learn to play classic games such as chess or board games like Monopoly, which can teach strategy, numeracy, competitiveness and perhaps even being a gracious winner or a good loser. Even as an adult you will be likely to play games. Have you ever played that one-player game at the petrol station, trying to hit exactly £20.00 and not go over to £20.01? Since the beginning of time, humans have played games, even back in ancient history. It strikes at the primal needs of challenge, competition and even the need to have fun.

Computer games are an extension of classic games, often having the same key elements, structures and core foundations.

A game of any type has certain fundamental features, whether it is something made up by friends in the playground, a classic board game or a commercial computer game designed by a team of professionals.

Essential Factors in a Game	
Objectives/goals/purpose	What are the players aiming towards? Do they need to 'reach the end' or 'score the most points'?
Rules	This may be as simple as each player taking turns or, in a computer game, applying the laws of gravity where a player cannot just 'fly away'.
Main characters (**protagonist/antagonist**)	Usually the player will be the 'hero' competing against the 'enemy', although some computer games have turned this on its head.
Story/narrative/backstory	A wider context in which the game exists to give it depth.
Good versus evil/struggle	A conflict between two opposing sides: a 'goodie' and a 'baddie'.
Objects/**pickups**	These are items which can be used; for example, playing pieces in chess which each have special meaning, or 'a heart' in a computer game to give the player extra health.
Winning and losing	It has to be possible to both win a game or lose a game – to win every time becomes boring; to lose every time is frustrating.
Achievement	To gain a sense of achievement from winning the game.
Replayability and longevity	A good game should stand the test of time and be able to be played more than once, and encourage a player to continue playing.
Challenge	An element of challenge where the player has to perhaps use their skills or intelligence to win or make further progress.
Environment	A world in which the game takes place, for example, a game board or a virtual world.

Although this is not an exhaustive list, it gives a foundation upon which the term 'game' can be built.

Let's apply some of these essential elements to Noughts and Crosses:

Objective	To get three of your symbols in a row.
Rules	You have to take turns; only use a nought or a cross; only play within the lines.
Main characters	Nought (protagonist) and cross (antagonist) – or the other way round, depending on which side you are playing.
Story	A battle of good versus evil, conflict, struggle.
Winning and losing	It is possible to win, lose or draw in this game.
Challenge	As this is a multiplayer game, it depends on the skill of the other player and the aim is to beat the other player.
Environment	This is a 3 x 3 grid.

There are enough significant characteristics listed that we can say that Noughts and Crosses is definitely a game! These factors are not only useful in deciding if something is a game or not, but by deconstructing them we can better understand games; and even consider which characteristics we would need to include if we were inventing a game of our own.

There are some additional factors that we can add to the list which are optional and more related to computer games:

Additional Factors

- escapism
- fun
- individual or social interaction
- competitiveness
- sound
- secrets
- supporting characters (in computer games, these are known as **NPCs** (non-playing characters) and usually provide guidance for the player)

A Very Brief History

The first computer games were made in the 1950s, although there are a lot of arguments over who actually invented them. Early games were monochrome (black and white) and relatively simple. *Tennis for Two*, which later became *Pong*, involves a bat at either side of the screen and hitting a dot (ball) across a line (net). Compared with the games of today, this may seem quite boring; however, it had all the elements of a modern game and proved to be very addictive and highly successful.

Over the next 30 years the market was flooded with ever-increasing technology, and each new release saw something new and innovative. Score tables, sound, **multiplayer** – all features that we take for granted today had to be invented and improved. This period saw some classic names in gaming emerge: Spectrum, Commodore, Atari, Amiga.

The early 1980s saw the explosion of interest in gaming with the release of the Nintendo Entertainment System and the Sega Master System. Home gaming overtook the previously popular arcades which went out of fashion. With the introduction of these consoles, and the marketing wars which went with them bringing the prices down, home gaming became affordable and desirable. This was the period where you did not play games – you 'played on the Nintendo'.

During the 2000s, we reached the seventh generation of consoles and games. The PC became an extremely powerful system capable of playing games; some PCs were even dedicated to that task, and the three console giants (Microsoft Xbox 360, Sony PlayStation 3 and Nintendo Wii) were developing bigger and better games and technology in order to be at the forefront of the market.

As already mentioned, the Wii revolutionized the console game playing by introducing the Wii Remote, a handheld device that mainly operated by movement, rather than the traditional buttons which had been around in various forms since the beginning of gaming. To compete with this, in 2010 the PlayStation Move was released, allowing Wii-like motion interaction with its own remotes. In the same year the Xbox Kinect became available which allows users to interact with their Xbox 360 console with no remotes at all – it all being done with body movements and voice commands, a huge step forward in technology.

The games market as a whole is massive – it is worth $65 billion in 2011, up from $62.7 billion in 2010 (Source: Reuters 06/06/11). Even though the industry took a hit during the recession in the late 2000s, as did most industries, it remained strong and promising throughout and is building back up. In terms of countries, Japan and the United States lead the market, with the United Kingdom in third place, and Canada, South Korea, China and other Western European countries not far behind.

The technology is changing swiftly, prices are falling and it is a very exciting area. **Glasses-less 3D** technology has already been used in the 3DS handheld from Nintendo, released in 2011 and with 3D televisions being developed, will this revolutionise gaming? Who knows what the next fascinating development may be after that.

1 Practicalities

Using computer games in education can add an extra dimension to teaching and create more effective learning. If we are honest about our subjects, there are always parts of the curriculum which are dull or difficult to teach. Using games could be a way to liven them up. Perhaps it could introduce a topic or reinforce key points. If there are concepts or ideas which pupils find difficult to grasp, using games could offer a different approach to delivering these ideas from an alternative angle.

As well as using them strategically to deliver the curriculum, you could also consider the moment you choose to employ them. Timing the use of games to coincide with a class flagging after lunch or on a Friday afternoon could make the teaching time more effective. Another way games could be used is as a reward. You could say to your pupils, 'If you do … (whatever it might be: work hard, complete a topic, etc.), then next lesson we will play games.' This could promote increased productivity; but, cunningly, the games played could also further pupil's learning, possibly without them realizing because they are having so much fun.

In this section, I will discuss using PCs, consoles and handheld and portable gaming devices. There are also sections on whether to use **online multiplayer** (page 17–18, 62–63), **steam and OnLive cloud gaming services** (page 15), **indie games** (page 16) and using **tablets** (such as iPads) and **smartphones** (such as iPhones, Android and Windows phones) (page 17).

Equipment in General

If you have not used computer games in teaching before, and perhaps have limited experience with games and equipment such as consoles, it is understandable that you may have concerns about introducing them into your lessons.

Do I need to buy the latest equipment?

Absolutely not! The latest equipment can be hugely expensive, as are the games you would also need to buy. If you are talking about consoles, the **hardware** could be at least £100-£200, if not more, and the most recent games are often released at £40. There is no need to go to this expense. You could buy older consoles, often available second hand, which can cost between £10-£40 and the games can be as little as £5 each, or purchased in deals such as five games for £20.

If you are considering buying a modern console, your choice is currently between offerings from Microsoft, Sony and Nintendo. The Xbox 360 has a version called the Elite (which is thin and black and was released in 2010); however, the previous version (which was hourglass-shaped and white and was released 2005) will run all of the same games and is cheaper. The PlayStation 3 (PS3) is the latest release from Sony; however, the PlayStation 2 (PS2) is still widely available, although fewer games are being released for it since the launch of the PS3. The Wii is the first of its kind; however, having been available for quite a while now, the original price (lower than the other two consoles) has fallen. With the release of the Wii U, which was first announced at the E3 games conference in 2011, it is likely that the price of original Wiis may fall further.

Alternatively, you could choose to use PCs and it is likely that your school's equipment will be powerful enough to run them, especially as you are not trying to play the latest, high-spec games. There are many free games available; sometimes it is just a matter of knowing where to look. Also you can support the UK games industry by encouraging indie developers who often provide their games for free, at a low cost or with an option for you to choose how much you pay.

Is it difficult to set up the equipment?

If you are using PCs, then the equipment will probably already be available in your school. You may be able to access the games online and you can therefore just start using them straight away. Two things you might need to consider are: a) your school's internet filter may block games, and b) some games need to be installed. With both aspects, if you speak to your IT Support, they should be able to help you.

If you choose to use a console, these are very easy to set up. You may have experience of setting up hardware in the past, where you have had to mess around with getting the right cables in the right places, tuning TVs to an obscure channel, having to adjust all sorts of settings and there being an element of crossing your fingers and hoping it works. With modern consoles, this is generally no longer the case and they are very easy to set up. **Sixth generation consoles**, which include the original Xbox and PlayStation 2, and later consoles can usually be set up with just two cables: a cable for the power (which goes in a wall socket) and a connection to the television (which will usually only fit in one port on the TV). As an alternative to a televison, you could connect the console to a projector which you could then project onto a whiteboard or wall, allowing a bigger screen and therefore making it easier for everyone in your class to see it. You may need to ask your IT Support or other technicians to advise you on the connections and cabling. You may also need speakers, depending on your projector setup.

To go online or to not go online?

You can connect computer games consoles to the internet; however, there would need to be a very good educational reason to do so which would negate the associated complication and risk. Connecting to the internet requires more set-up, and you must have or buy an online account for that network. It can also make the gaming unpredictable, as you never know what other gamers may be playing online, or what they might say or do. I would advise never to connect the console to the internet for teaching.

Will IT Support be annoyed with me for giving them more work?

It depends on your IT Support team, but I doubt it. In fact you are likely to find that they are enthusiastic to help. They are likely to be very supportive of your initiative in using games in your teaching and quite excited about the prospect of bringing this field of computing into education.

In addition, think about getting your Head of ICT or other ICT teachers involved. They are also likely to be excited about using games in teaching and willing to advise or even help out.

✳Preparing and Running Lessons Using Computer Games

The key to lessons involving computer games – just like any lesson that goes beyond the norm and the bog-standard – is to think it through in advance. This will result in a smoother lesson where you are in control, and one which your pupils and *you* will enjoy.

One of the most important aspects of using games is defining *why* you are using them – even if it is just to yourself. This will allow you to be clearer about the focus and therefore the structure of the lesson. Is this a learning opportunity? If so, what is the desired learning outcome? What should the pupils leave the room thinking about, knowing about or understanding that they didn't when they entered? Is it to reinforce previous learning or to try a different way of learning? Consider how you will ensure that the learning is clear, as well as fun. Or is it being used mostly as a treat? If so, how will you make sure there is something core underpinning the exercise, rather than just being an excuse for the pupils to let down their hair – well, not entirely!

How can I ensure learning is taking place with all this fun going on?

You may explain the lesson before the pupils begin to use the games what you are going to do and why. From this you could set homework for pupils to prepare for the lesson using games. For example, if you are going to play a specific game, you could ask your pupils to research it, perhaps finding out the rating, the main characters and so on, so they know a bit about it beforehand. You can decide whether to make a rule about no plot spoilers if it is a more recent game, as some pupils may be playing it and not want the ending spoilt (endings can often be found on the internet).

Alternatively, you may wish the lesson to be self-contained. As the pupils enter the room, the learning objectives could be written on the board (or on flip-chart paper attached to the wall if the board is in use for displaying the game). In your introduction, highlight the learning objectives and explain what the children should be thinking about in this lesson and what they should get out of it.

You could set them a task or worksheet to do during the lesson, for times when they are not playing. This can also be good for keeping them occupied while they are watching others play. One task could be watching out for and discussing a particular aspect of the game. If you set the deadline for the task as the end of the lesson and make it a bit tricky or thought-provoking, the pupils will have to work hard in times when they are not playing to complete it. If this work is based on the game, they will need to be aware of what is going on in the class as well as doing the work.

For a discussion-based lesson, you could periodically pause the game, perhaps between levels (or similar), and open up the floor for discussion of what the children have seen. Then continue playing and repeat this sequence a few times.

Another method is to identify aspects your pupils should watch out for in the game during the lesson and then set them homework to discuss it, research it further, answer questions or somehow apply what they have seen to a piece of work.

Are the lessons difficult to manage?

Not at all, due to your good planning. Consider how the pupils will play the game. Will there be a tournament where everyone gets at least one go with a winner at the end? Will just some of them get a chance to play? Will the game be played by someone else as a demonstration for the class to watch, perhaps to begin a discussion? Will the games take up all of the lesson or just part of it? If you plan exactly how the playing of the games will happen, this will make the execution of it much easier. Also think about how long the playing of the games will last, taking into account swapping between players, discussion and explanations. Leave plenty of time spare as it may take longer than you anticipate, especially to get going at the beginning as the pupils are likely to be excited when they realize what will be in their lesson.

What about the layout of the room?

Think through your space. If you are using a console, it is likely you will be setting up the equipment at the front of the classroom, showing images through a large TV or projecting onto a whiteboard. The console will need to be near the projector, power and screen, with the controllers extending further into the classroom for the pupils to use. What I normally do is establish a 'no go' area. I mark an area around the screen, console, any trailing wires and any other equipment apart from the controllers.

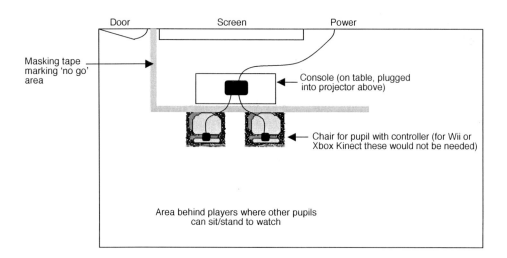

I mark the area very simply with white masking tape on the floor and explain to the pupils before they enter the room that one toe over the line and we stop and put the games away. By putting the responsibility onto the pupils, they are more likely to respond to these rules. You have provided this special lesson for them; but if they do not follow the rules, they only have themselves to blame for the consequences. I have always found that pupils are so pleased to be using the games equipment that they are happy to follow the rules. Once they are established, you can concentrate on running your fun lesson.

Also consider where pupils will sit or stand when they are not playing. Rearrange the tables if necessary.

Decide whether you will turn off the lights and, if you are able to control each bank of lights independently, which you will turn off (the front to see the screen more clearly) and which you will leave on (the back to discourage messing around by non-players).

How often should I use games in learning and teaching?

As often as you wish, but not too much that they become mundane. I am certainly not suggesting you should use games every lesson or that they should replace any of your core teaching methods. It is more that they are a special tool which you can use when they will be effective and useful. Any more than this and they will lose their magic and become ineffectual. You may wish to use them once, or once a term, or once a fortnight – whatever works for you and your pupils and the curriculum you are delivering.

Also, don't think of games as being a single flat option, as they are not – there are so many opportunities available to you. There are many different types and styles of games and gaming which you can use. In one lesson you may choose to play a commercial game on a console and devote a whole lesson to it and then, a couple of weeks later, you may ask pupils to end the lesson by using a game on the PC as a plenary. Although these are both computer games, they are very different experiences and broaden the range of tools in your toolbox.

How do I ensure all the pupils are included in the activity?

The key is preparation. If you want to make sure that all of your pupils are involved at some stage, draw up a list or create a **tournament structure**. This could be done beforehand or at the beginning of the lesson by names drawn out of a hat. If the pupils know they will have a fair turn, they will be more willing to watch others.

Make sure you have plenty of time for the activity, especially if you would like everyone to be involved. What happens if you overrun? If you choose a lesson that occurs just before a break or lunch, might your pupils be willing to stay in for a little time to complete the activity? This is obviously better than overrunning into another lesson or over the end of the day when pupils may need to catch buses or are being collected.

Consider what your pupils will be doing while some are playing. Just asking them to watch passively is likely to leave them restless, talkative and potentially misbehaving. If you ask them to actively engage in what is happening, however, they should maintain their focus. Prepare worksheets for them to complete while others are playing. For each game, give those watching a 'focus' topic for them to discuss afterwards. You could even add an element of competition: divide the watching pupils into two groups and whichever team makes the most perceptive comments or completes the worksheet to a high standard gains house points or your school's equivalent.

When dealing with playing games, the most apparent issue is motor skills but also consider other factors involved in playing such as hearing or sight. Think about any pupils in your class with special needs and ensure they can be included in the activity. If you are in doubt about how to do this, check the pupil's SEN record or speak to your SENCO or equivalent. Remember you can also always ask the pupil. They are the ones best placed to understand any condition they may have and may already have a solution for over-coming any issues. I once taught a pupil with very limited use of hands and arms; however, he had developed a method of putting his bag on his knee and resting the controller on top – and could beat everyone in the class at most games!

PCs

PCs used for gaming somewhat stemmed from Ataris and Amigas in the 1980s, and Commodores, Sinclairs, BBCs and Apples before that. At first PCs were mostly thought of as being for **casual games** – I am sure you will have momentarily succumbed to *Solitaire* or *Minesweeper* if you have a Windows PC. With the release of bigger games such as *Diablo* (1996) and *The Sims* (2000), the PC began to be treated as a suitable **platform** for gaming, and nowadays it competes equally with consoles, although with a notably smaller share of the market.

You are likely to have suitable equipment for playing PC games in your school already. Although your PCs might not be powerful enough to play the most recent releases, they are likely to be able to cope with most. If you are unsure, ask your IT Support. Look at the **system requirements** for the game you are considering – often they will state the minimum for running it and the ideal spec which will eliminate any jerky graphics or lag in the game. Consider the **processor speed, RAM and graphics card**.

Steam and OnLive

Steam is an online game platform made by Valve (who have also published the popular game series Half-Life, Portal and Left 4 Dead). Steam allows users to purchase games from a list of well over a thousand, download them straight to the computer, save games to the Steam Cloud (allowing users to log onto Steam and access their saved games anywhere) and play multiplayer including text and voice chat. Steam is fast becoming the main way to buy and play games on a computer, rather than going to a shop and buying a physical copy. They often have huge discounts, even on new and popular titles. Visit www.steampowered.com for more information.

OnLive is another games service which utilizes cloud technology. The biggest difference between these two is that games purchased through Steam are downloaded onto the user's computer and then can be played, whereas OnLive games are streamed through the internet onto the user's computer. Steam games may take time to download and need space on the hard drive to save them, but when played they only use the computer's resources. Comparatively, OnLive requires minimal hard drive space, can be played immediately (without waiting for the whole game to download and install onto the computer), but needs a very good internet connection for the smooth running of the game.

As internet connections become faster and more reliable, it will be interesting to see if digital game sales will overtake traditional boxed game sales, and whether download or streaming models will become the norm. Visit www.onlive.com for more information.

Consoles

Consoles are computers which have been specifically designed to play games on, although some modern consoles also act as media centres, being able to stream TV, play DVDs and blu-rays and access the internet. If you are buying a console for your school, consider if these additional features might be useful in your classroom.

The **seventh generation of consoles** are Xbox 360, PlayStation 3 and Wii, although older consoles are available and are usually much cheaper, as are the games. The predecessors to the Xbox 360 (Xbox, known as 'Original' Xbox) and PlayStation 3 (PlayStation 2) can generally be bought second-hand from computer game stores. Earlier consoles than these can still be very useful for education, although the older the console, the more expensive it becomes.

When using a console in school, make sure it is kept safe after use. Either remove and lock it away, or, if left in the classroom, use secure fastenings to ensure it cannot be moved. Although we do not want to think any pupil might be light-fingered with it, it is better to be safe than sorry.

Indie Games

Indie games are ones which are released to the public but not published on a **commercial label**. They are often designed and built by one person (often known as 'bedroom coders') or a small team, made as a hobby and not expected to recoup much financial reward for the creator. They are often free, although some have a very low price or allow the purchaser to choose how much they pay. As such, indie games can vary widely in quality. A high number are very good quality. Minecraft is the 'king of the indies' with over 11 million players worldwide (as of August 2011, but this number is growing rapidly). Some indies get release opportunities on larger networks such as Xbox Live, notable games including Braid, Limbo and Super Meat Boy. There is, of course, the other end of the scale, and some very poor games. However, it is hoped that these games will not be played, will not be talked about positively and will fade into obscurity. The indie market tends to include a high number of clones, where individual developers or smaller teams have tried to copy successful games, and these can often be quite disastrous. Also there are the inevitable 'fart-simulators' which seem to be continuously released and appeal to people with a particular sense of humour.

Indie games can be found all over the internet, but good sources include www. indiegames.com and www.tigsource.com. There are also indie releases on Steam (see page 15) at www.steampowered.com and **console networks Xbox Live and PlayStation Network**.

Handhelds and Portables

Handheld, portable gaming has been well liked since the 1980s and rose to huge popularity with Nintendo's GameBoy. The current handheld gaming systems on the market are from Nintendo, the DS and the 3DS, and from Sony, the PlayStation Vita (replacing the PlayStation Portable (PSP)). The 3DS is notable as it is the first handheld to offer glasses-less 3D graphics, although this has obviously raised the price. The DS is still considered a 'current' device if you wish to buy any and is cheaper than the 3DS. It has been said that the PS Vita provides a lot of technology in a small package, with six axis motion control, **multi-touch pads** and multiple cameras, high-speed internet connection and cross play, which links games to a PS3 console, meaning you can play a game on console then seamlessly continue playing on the Vita on the move.

Tablets and Smartphones

In addition to handheld gaming systems, Smartphones (e.g., iPhones, Androids and Windows 7 phones) and tablets (e.g., iPad) are beginning to be considered real contenders in the gaming market. At first they were merely seen as casual gaming devices and not particularly taken as a serious threat to the industry. However, there has been a massive rise in popularity, with games like *Angry Birds*, *Fruit Ninja* and the Zynga family of games, including *Words with Friends* and *Farmville*. There are also a lot of large games being ported to these platforms, from well-established companies such as EA and Rockstar.

Networked Gaming

Playing games over a network can add an extra interesting dimension to gaming and one which we, as teachers, can use and adapt. This multiplayer aspect can allow pupils in a class to compete against each other or work together. In addition, they could compete with pupils in different classes, or even create links with other schools and other groups external to the school.

PCs connected together in a single space (like a classroom) is called a **Local Area Network (LAN)**. If these PCs are in isolation – that is, they are not connected to the internet – then they can only communicate with each other. This means only the people sat at those computers would be able to play the games with each other and chat.

Consoles usually offer multiplayer; for example, four controllers can be used simultaneously in the Xbox 360 and Wii and seven in PlayStation 3. However, for more players, Xbox consoles can be connected in a LAN similar to PCs (and without the internet). This is known as **system link**.

PCs and consoles can be connected to the internet to open up wider possibilities, and players can play and chat with people from all around the world. However, there are risks associated with this (please see eSafety on page 19).

For any networking, you are strongly advised to speak to your IT Support and Head of ICT – they will hopefully be very keen and excited to help!

Health and Safety

Bringing new equipment into your class can incur some health and safety risks, albeit not severe. If you are asked to carry out a risk assessment on your activity, or need to identify health and safety risks on your lesson plan, consider including the following:

Risk	Preventative Action
Tripping over trailing cables	Cables are kept as neatly and as flat as possible; fixed to the floor with tape. Area has been marked out on floor with masking tape which pupils must not enter.
Use of electrical equipment	Power sockets will not be overloaded and, where possible, extension cables and multi-blocks will not be used; advice of IT Support will be sought.
Use of digital displays	Pupils will be seated at a suitable distance from the screen so as not to damage their eyes and will not be required to concentrate on digital images for too long; appropriate breaks will be taken.
Use of lighting	Lights may be switched off or dimmed during play, but will be turned on for pupils entering and exiting the room and when pupils are asked to move around; will ensure there is sufficient light for the teacher to monitor pupils safety and behaviour and that they do not risk falling or tripping because of the reduced light.
Over-excitement/ misbehaviour during activity	Pupils to be clearly briefed on activity and rules given; the teacher to monitor carefully and intervene if any behaviour is unacceptable or indicates that it may become so.
Danger of Wii remote being thrown during play	**Wrist straps** always to be used; pupils briefed that activity will stop if wrist straps not used.
Over-exertion or injury during physical games (such as Wii or Kinect)	Warm-up exercises to be used; pupils to wear suitable clothing; suitable breaks to be taken.

If you have pupils with special needs, these should also be taken into consideration. Be especially aware of epilepsy, which could be triggered by flashing lights, and consider choosing a game which does not cause that risk – it should be stated on the box, in the manual or in the intro before the game starts. Check this before choosing to use it and, if in doubt, do not take any risks and select a different game.

eSafety

As soon as you introduce an 'opening up' of technology to a wider audience, potential risks begin to rear their ugly heads. This is especially true once it goes beyond the virtual boundaries of your school, even if it is just to allow access to your pupils at home, but particularly if it is open to anyone on the internet to join. Think very carefully if you want to try network gaming and decide how you will go about it and what the consequences might be. If you want to purchase games from a network, such as the **Arcade** games through Xbox Live, you could go online to buy them but then play them with your pupils offline.

Although pupils are likely to have access to the whole internet, unfiltered and unfettered at home, and probably on their phones wherever they go as well, as soon as they use a tool from their school to communicate and play with others, there is an implied 'sanctioning' by the school. Therefore, if there are instances of cyberbullying, virus spreading or other incidents, the school may hold some responsibility. In addition, I am sure you, as a conscientious teacher, would not want to have on your conscience that you encouraged a pupil to use something which then led them into harm.

I would advise that all network gaming for pupils is done on a stand-alone network built inside the school, through your school's **VLE** or on a carefully set-up, very secure, school-run sub-network which is administrated by yourself and your IT Support team. In addition, when running anything like this, let your Head of ICT and someone in Senior Management (perhaps the Child Protection Officer) know, so that they can support you should something arise. They are likely to be supportive of your exciting initiative and grateful that you have kept them informed, and they are best placed to give you advice and guidance.

2 Educational Games Online

There are many teaching resources on the internet and a good proportion of them involve games. A lot have been made to cover specific topics which will be useful to you in your subject teaching. The great thing about them is that they are FREE, accessible online (meaning you and your pupils can access them on any **internet-enabled computer**) and made for schools, meaning there should be no inappropriate content.

Suggestions for Online Games Sites

These suggestions are suitable for a variety of subjects and key stages:

- **BBC Bitesize KS2, KS3, KS4 and KS5**

  www.bbc.co.uk/bitesize

  BBC Bitesize is an excellent site for teaching resources and has some brilliant games especially made for it. It was originally built as a GCSE revision site but has since expanded to KS5 and also English, Maths and Science for KS2 and KS3. The games can be found by going into the level of education you want, then either using the Games link on the left, or within the specific subject you want. These games could be used as a starter or plenary, a break between activities in the lesson – or even set as homework.

- **BBC Schools: Games sections for ages 4 to 16+**

  www.bbc.co.uk/schools/games

  Containing a wide range of games, this site is divided into age groups: 4–7, 7–11, 11–16 and 16+. The games can be used by selecting the spinners on the home page or the dropdown list underneath. On the left is a link for teachers, where not only can you get more information about the game provided but access to more resources or links to other great sites.

- **Website of the Nobel Prize: Games section**

  www.nobelprize.org/educational

  This website contains games and simulations based on the achievements of Nobel Prize winners. This includes Astrophysics, Human Rights and Literature. Although a lot of these topics are at quite a high level, using games makes them very accessible and more enjoyable for pupils.

Suitable for: Science, English, History and PSHE-type subjects

- **Arcadu**

  www.arcadu.com

  The aim of Arcadu is to combine answering questions with playing games. The questions span a variety of curriculum subject areas and are suitable for primary and secondary school age pupils. In addition, you can register as the teacher and be sent detailed reports which show progress. You can add your own content, so you can tailor questions to your pupils' learning. There is a subscription fee, but also a free thirty day trial for you to try.

  Suitable for: Maths, English, Science, ICT, History, Geography, RE, PE, Design and Technology, MFL

- **Teachable**

  www.teachable.net

  Teachable is a website which contains resources made by teachers, many of which are games. The sections are separated into ages and subjects and are easy to navigate.

  Suitable for: Maths, English, Science, MFL, Geography, History, Art, Business, Design & Technology, ICT, Music, PE, RE, Psychology

Another interesting website you might find useful is www.topmarks.co.uk. It calls itself an educational search engine and allows you to click on subjects on the left side and provides links to a wide selection of educational websites, many including games but also containing other teaching resources you may find useful.

Below are some subject specific sites you might wish to check out:

- **Maths:** www.mangahigh.com

  Manga High allows teachers to set up pupils in classes and set them challenges which the pupils can take part in online. You can then view reports of the results and analyse the data produced. The site has been developed by an experienced team of mathematicians and game specialists, and encourages game-based learning with the aim of making learning and revising Maths enjoyable.

- **English:** www.teachit.co.uk

  This website provides resources for teaching English. There is a wealth of materials available, and for games click on Whizzy Things on the left of the page. There are games such as *Anagrams, Scramble, Interactive Fridge Magnets* and other inspiring word games.

- **Chemistry:** www.creative-chemistry.org.uk

  Creative Chemistry provides resources for KS3, KS4 and KS5. As well as worksheets and other resources, there are several games. Either use the links on the main page or click on Fun Stuff in the top right corner. There you will find a range of games, interactive crosswords and word searches.

- **Physics:** www.physicsgames.net

  Physics lends itself to games really well and this website is crammed full of interesting **mini-games** which look at a variety of physics concepts and could be incorporated into lessons as a fun starter, motivating plenary or as a treat for good behaviour during a lesson.

- **Biology:** www.biogames.info

  Biogames has a huge range of games based on biology topics from anatomy to viruses. These games could be used as a nice starter to get pupils interested in a particular topic, to remind them of previous learning, or as a basis for an activity; for example, pupils might play a game about cells then, as a group, create a presentation on what they have learned.

- **Geography:** http://mapzone.ordnancesurvey.co.uk/mapzone/games.html

  This website has a great selection of Geography resources and on this games page there are four games. The first two are quite traditional but, being interactive, add an extra element to the crossword and hangman. The other two ask pupils to use their map-reading skills and other geography knowledge to solve puzzles and win the game. The first two could be used as short activities; the other two might take a little longer.

- **ICT:** www.teach-ict.com/quizhome.htm

  This site has excellent resources, a lot of which can be used for free or an annual subscription can be paid for access to all the resources on the site. This link will take you to the quizzes section where you can play a huge range of pre-made games or even make your own.

- **History:** www.schoolhistory.co.uk/games

  School History gives you a wide selection of resources, from downloadable worksheets to interactive whiteboard activities. Going directly to this link you will find a selection of games on a huge range of History topics from Ancient to Modern.

- **Languages:** www.francais-extra.co.uk/frxmflgames/frenchgamesmenu.htm

  Français Extra has resources for French and this section contains a variety of games, both word based and visual for practising, revising and remembering words and language.

- **Music:** www.agame.com/games/music/music.html, www.musicgames.co

  These two websites both contain a huge collection of music games. They cover all sorts of styles including rock and hip hop and use different skills such as asking pupils to press buttons in rhythm, harmonize different parts of music and understanding instruments.

For more suggestions, please visit www.karen-anderson.org.

These suggestions are just to get you started – there are many more available and more can appear at any time, thus is the nature of the internet. If you discover any useful sites, please share your information on my website.

Using Online Games for Starters and Plenaries

These types of games are generally short and are often tailored to particular topics being studied. However, a game may not cover the topic specifically – therefore, always try it out before you ask your pupils to play it. For example, the game may be revision for a GCSE course, but depending on the exam board, the content or approach may be slightly different. In general, however, they will cover the main topics.

Using these types of games for starters can help focus the class, get the pupils thinking about the topic to be studied that lesson or even to work as a team. Using it as a plenary can be a great way to review learning, the game often automatically checking progress as the pupils progress.

If you have access to ICT, you may wish the pupils to play the games individually or in pairs, giving house points or similar to the top three scores, or those who have the highest score within a set amount of time, for example, five minutes. Alternatively you could play the game as a class. By showing the game on a board or screen through a projector, the pupils can play as one group or be split into two competing teams, with the winning team being declared at the end of each term or half-term. Depending on the game, you could have your pupils working together to play the game or you could have a 'hotspot' moment where each pupil takes a turn each lesson to be the person playing the game. If pupils are in teams, they can support the pupils playing, perhaps one from each team each lesson and the scores are totalled for the team and prizes awarded at regular intervals. If this method is used across a department, you could even introduce a mini awards ceremony for the winning team throughout the department for the term.

3 Activities

This section contains numerous activities that make use of games in a variety of educational ways. They are organised by subject and skill; however, you can also locate them using the two matrices at the back of this book.

Subjects

Computer games can be used in all subjects as they are incredibly versatile and adaptable. There are many aspects to them, types available and ways of using them. Listed below are just a few to get you started.

Art and Design

Art and design are areas which lend themselves well to computer games as they are an integral part of the medium. As such, there are numerous opportunities in which to use games, either by studying them or using them as a basis for an activity.

Activity: Investigating Art Styles

Games: Examples include *Braid* (Xbox Arcade), *Ilo Milo* (Xbox Arcade), *Bioshock* (Xbox 360), *Limbo* (Xbox Arcade), *Wet* (Xbox 360), *XIII* (original Xbox), *Little Big Planet* (PS3)

Duration: One lesson or a short project

Computer games often have very distinctive styles of art. This might be **genre**-specific, creating a mood or recreating a certain theme. Each of the games listed are examples which have notable art styles. For example, *XIII* is in a comic-book style, complete with sound effect bubbles like *Pow!* and *Smash!* and scenes are drawn inside comic book frames. *Bioshock*, on the other hand, is set in an underwater world built in the 1920s and its artwork is remarkable for recreating the art deco style in the architecture and decor.

   Pupils could look at different styles of art in games and discuss the differences between them and also the artistic fundamentals on which they are based. This could be done by splitting the class into small groups, giving each group two or three games to

---

analyse and then each group should create a presentation for the rest of the class based on what they have found out. The games could be played live in class or pupils could be asked to find clips of in-game action on the internet.

Extension: Pupils could be asked to choose one of the styles they have been investigating and recreate a classic piece of art in the style of that game. For example, a pupil could be allocated Van Gogh's *Sunflowers* and the game *Limbo* and hopefully the end result would be sunflowers in greyscale, looking very eerie and possibly withered.

Activity:	Minecraft Sculptures
Games:	*Minecraft* (PC indie)
Duration:	Long project, possibly as homework/own time

Minecraft is an indie game where the world is made up of cube blocks. Although the graphics are quite rough and **pixelated**, the game is a really useful educational tool as it is completely open and has no storyline – the player creates their own storyline. This means that the player can move anywhere around the environment and has freedom over what they do.

The essence of the game is to mine and craft. The player can mine blocks and collect the material, whether it be stone, wood, gems or any of the materials available. They can then craft more materials by combining them. As they progress they can build tools, ovens, glass and even bake cakes. It is a very easy game to learn and can be very involving. *Minecraft* can be set up on a **server** (which can be run by IT Support at your school) and then only your pupils could have access. Also you can set the rules; for example, you can decide whether to remove all enemies and to allocate protected areas of land to each player.

For this particular activity, each pupil could have the aim of building a sculpture in *Minecraft*. You may wish to make this brief more focused, depending on your pupils and whether you are tying this into another project. The pupils must go out and find the materials they want, perhaps they will want certain textures or colours, and they might need to craft in order to get the exact right material. Then they should gradually build their sculpture. For pupils to do a good job of this, it is likely to be an extended project, You may wish to set it as ongoing homework where pupils can access the *Minecraft* server from home or in their spare time at school. Perhaps at the end of the term you could give some class time to looking at the finished pieces, with perhaps a mini awards ceremony. This also gives a firm deadline for completing the sculptures.

Extension: *Minecraft* is often compared to being 'digital Lego'. By providing pupils with Lego bricks they could attempt to create a version of the digital sculpture in the real world.

Activity:	Are Games Art?
Games:	Examples (either played, videos of, or box art) would be useful such as *Okami* (PS2, Wii), *Beautiful Katamari* (Xbox 360), *Electroplankton* (DS), *Final Fantasy* series and movies (various), *Flower* (PS3), *Ico* (PS2, PS3), *Braid* (Xbox Arcade, PlayStation Network, PC, Mac), *Machinarium* (PlayStation Network, PC, Mac, Wii, iPad, Smartphones), *Child of Eden* (Xbox 360, PS3)
Duration:	One lesson

Are games art? This is a question which has been long debated and still rages with no definitive answer. This is a great opportunity for your pupils to consider what 'art' is, and what does and does not fit into that category.

At the beginning of the lesson, before pupils know what they are going to be investigating, they could be asked to get into groups and write down five criteria which define something as art. They could look at classic art (paintings, sculpture, etc.) and see if their criteria work, refining them if needed. Then they could look at the game examples and analyse their artistic qualities. They could also consider the purpose of games, messages which are conveyed and the audience (both the developers target audience and others who may play the games). They should then apply their criteria to each game analysed. In drawing their conclusions they should decide whether they think games are art and justify their reasoning.

Extension: The question of what is art can be extended to other media and forms of design and discussions could extend to question whether film (including Hollywood blockbusters), cars or comic books.

Activity: The Real World as a Game

Games: None

Duration: One lesson (or homework)

Each computer game often has its own art style, whether it is trying to look realistic, cartoony or recreate a distinctive look. In this activity pupils could aim to take that style and apply it to their own artwork.

Each pupil could be asked to choose a game (or the games could be drawn out of a hat). They must then find examples of artwork from that game (on the internet, either in images or videos). Their task is then to draw something from the real world in the style of their allocated game art. This might be a portrait, a still life, a scene (like a high street) or something else where they are taking their inspiration from a game and applying it to real world images.

Extension: As well as creating their artwork, pupils could be asked to write an accompanying description explaining their piece and what techniques they have used to incorporate the game art style.

Activity: Box Art

Games: None, although game boxes would be useful, rather than just images

Duration: One lesson

The artwork of computer game boxes is very different to in-game art as it has to fulfil many more functions. It must represent the game inside, attract a buyer's attention, tempt the buyer into purchasing it, portray elements of genre, clearly state the name of the game, and also meet requirements such as an **age classification**.

Pupils could look at box art and discuss the different styles and techniques used to fulfil these purposes. They could look at how genre is shown, how colour is used and how mood is conveyed. Their analysis could result in a comparison of three game boxes or, alternatively, a set of guidelines for creating a game box for a certain type of game (family, **first-person shooter, strategy**, and so on).

Extension: Pupils could be told about a new (fictional) game which is to be released called *KryptoSmash* and that they have been commissioned to create the box art for it. To give the task more focus (or tie it in with other projects), you could define the genre, style of game or audience, or leave that open for the pupils to decide.

Activity: 3D in a 2D Medium

Games: None (although some examples of 3D game artwork would be useful)

Duration: One lesson

Computer games are often drawn in 3D. However, they only exist in a 2D medium because a screen is flat. So HOW do games achieve the look of 3D when they only have two dimensions with which to work?

Pupils should look at 3D games graphics and try to determine what makes them appear 3D. They could look at characters, objects and environments. They should be investigating lighting and shading, perspective, texture and other similar aspects. As an end product they could produce a short informative video explaining their discoveries, as though it were a piece on a television show.

Extension: Game graphics are made up of **polygons**. The more polygons used, the more realistic graphics look. Ask your pupils to look at graphics from older games (from consoles such as Commodore, Spectrum, Atari and Amiga) – they should be able to find images of these on the internet. Can they see the polygons? Can they see how the images are made up? Why do they think polygons are used? How do these older images compare to those in modern graphics?

Business Studies

The games industry is an interesting area of study, but also there are numerous games which simulate business well and can give pupils a practical understanding while having fun.

Activity: Games Simulating Business 1

Games: *Game Dev Story* (iPad/iPhone)

Duration: Ongoing project, possibly as homework

In *Game Dev Story* players run a computer games studio. They start with a small budget and two employees, and aim to make their company successful, popular and profitable. They must decide what platform they will design for, which genre of games and how they will advertise their games. They can hire and fire staff, allocate training and choose whether to use their own staff or hire in external talent for different parts of each game. There are also trade exhibitions, game critics and the occasional power cut. It is a very good simulation of real-world business. The games are run over 20 game years and can take quite some time to play; however, can be saved at any point.

Pupils could each be asked to set up a studio in *Game Dev Story* and, at the end of 20 game years, report back how much profit they have made. The pupil's company with the most profit could be the 'winner'.

Extension: Pupils could write a business report about their business, summarizing their business as though reporting to their shareholders.

Activity: Games Simulating Business 2

Games: *Football Manager* series (PC/Mac)

Duration: One lesson, ongoing as a series of starts or plenaries, or as homework

There are a number of sports games which allow you to create a football team, but they are mostly focused on playing the matches, tactics and are centred on the sport. *Football Manager* introduced a different style of game, where the crux of the game was all about managing the business of the teams: buying and selling players, managing investment from the board and dealing with the media.

Extension: This game can be linked to a study of real-world football teams and comparing the pupils' achievements with their teams with the actual teams.

Activity: Games Simulating Business 3

Games: *Rollercoaster Tycoon* series (PC)

Duration: Ongoing project, possibly as homework

In these games, the players are tasked with creating and running a theme park. They can set out the layout, choose what entertainment they will have and even design some of the rides themselves. Guests enter the park and the more they enjoy themselves and spend money, the more successful the theme park is. Players need to think about things like bins, lighting, benches and toilets. They need to make sure the paths connect rides together logically so guests do not become lost and unhappy. They must also make sure the park is safe. If the park is successful, it can be expanded; but the player also needs to consider maintenance costs to keep the rides working, security guards, and handymen to empty the bins and mow the lawns.

Pupils could be asked to run a theme park, individually or in pairs, for a set amount of time. At the deadline, pupils should screenshot their final totals and the most successful theme park, with the most profit, is the 'winner'.

Extension: The final profit totals could be presented in a report to the shareholders, with other information including any statistics gathered, what rides were in their park, how much it is liked, and perhaps also an estimate of how much the whole property is worth, if they were to sell it.

Activity: Analysis of the Games Industry
Games: None
Duration: One lesson or a basis for a larger project

The games industry is a fascinating one to analyse and study. There is a whole range of sizes of business, from sole traders who create games single-handedly in their bedrooms to massive commercial enterprises. Whether a company is a success is dependent on many factors, including the amount of capital available, the products produced and marketing, which are similar to other business areas. However, in the games industry there are extra issues, such as the mood of the public, controversy (avoiding it or courting it) and **intellectual property (IP)** – what to do with popular or classic characters or series: continue them, stop them, change them? There are also the choices of which platform to develop for: exclusively for one or across them all? Will the product be transferable to console, motion controllers or portable gaming devices? Should the business create hardware or software or both?

Pupils could analyse the industry as a whole or work on case studies of large companies. There are opportunities to study mergers, splits and takeovers as they happen quite often.

Pupils could also look at the marketing strategy of console releases, including how they are announced and demonstrated, what times of the year they go on sale and the progress of sales figures from early adopters to later purchasers. An interesting case study is the release of the seventh generation consoles: Nintendo Wii, Xbox 360 and PlayStation 3. Pupils could compare the functionality provided by these consoles, their release dates, their original retail prices and their sales figures across time.

Extension: Branding and advertising are also interesting areas of the games industry to investigate. Pupils could consider how certain colour schemes, sound clips and mascots are used across hardware and software and the different target markets for which they are intended. For a controversial discussion that is likely to get your pupils fired up, you could show your pupils an advert for an 18-rated game and suggest that this game is designed for adults and there is NO WAY younger teenagers and children could be interested in it!

Drama

Computer games are often about characters, action and movement and therefore can be a rich source of ideas for activities in Drama.

Activity: Cut Scene 1

Games: A game's cut scene such as *Mass Effect* (Xbox, PC), *The Secret of Monkey Island* (PC, Mac, Xbox Arcade, PlayStation Network, iPhone, iPad), *Batman Arkham Asylum* (Xbox 360, PS3, PC), *Metal Gear Solid 4: Guns of the Patriots* (PS3)

Duration: One lesson

The majority of games have **cut scenes,** which are animated sequences either to tell a part of the story or to progress the action. There is usually one at the beginning, explaining the premise of the game and introducing the main character and the situation; then they are used through the game. They could be used in a structured way – at the beginning or end of every level – or neatly woven into the game itself. Pupils could be asked to watch a cut scene and then recreate it. This could be at the beginning of a game or at an interesting point in the story where something dramatic happens. They will need to think about characterization and how they will show their environment (e.g., how will the audience know they are on a spaceship?). If necessary they can make amendments (e.g., add in dialogue to comment on how long they have been in space), as long as they still tell the same story and end in the same place ready for the player to take over.

Extension: To add extra layers of complexity to the challenge, pupils could be given a restriction, such as only being allowed one prop, or asked to change the setting, such as the same story and dialogue but now set on a hot beach.

Activity: Cut Scene 2

Games: A game's cut scene such as *Mass Effect* (Xbox, PC), *The Secret of Monkey Island* (PC, Mac, Xbox Arcade, PlayStation Network, iPhone, iPad), *Batman Arkham Asylum* (Xbox 360, PS3, PC), *Metal Gear Solid 4: Guns of the Patriots* (PS3)

Duration: One to two lessons

A second option with cut scenes is to write 'what happens next'. Having watched the cut scene, pupils must take those characters and that situation and decide on the next piece of story. Most cut scenes end on a cliff-hanger or where characters are just about to step into some action. This should provide pupils with a good starting point for their scene. Pupils should first plan and script their mini-play, then rehearse and finally perform it.

Extension: To add an extra layer of challenge, you could give pupils some set phrases, actions or emotions to include in their mini-plays. These could be general, as in all must include a choreographed (and safe!) fight scene. Alternatively, the challenge could be more random, as names of props, emotions and lines of dialogue are put into a hat for each group to draw out.

Activity: Alternative Ending

Games: *Dead Island* (Xbox 360, PS3, PC) (could also use the trailer), *Alan Wake* (Xbox 360), *Fable* series (Xbox 360, PC), *Halo* (Xbox 360)

Duration: One lesson

Large, modern games often have interesting and complex storylines. These can often be acquired on the internet, in **walkthroughs** or by purchasing a **strategy guide book** for the game. The story will have a set of characters, an environment in which everything takes place and a plot which will come to a resolution at the end.

Pupils could be asked to look at this storyline and come up with an alternative ending. It may be useful for them to see the beginning of the game and some of the gameplay to get a feel for it. Then they could read through the story and devise a different ending.

This could also be a good activity for English and even History (if using a game based on a historical setting).

English/Literacy

Despite computer games having a reputation for not being positive for literacy development, in fact quite the opposite can be true. Many computer games require the player to read on screen and use words in order to progress further in the game, perhaps by choosing the words their character will say and seeing the result of their choice. In addition, all games have a plot or storyline, some being quite interesting and complex with flashbacks or time jumps. Colloquial speech might be used or regional accents.

At their core, computer games are stories, creative writing, told in a mostly visual medium (like film) but allowing the player to interact or control the story. Some games even allow the players to write their own stories or, by choosing a series of options, determine the outcome for the characters.

Activity: Analysing Storyline

Games: *Halo Reach* (Xbox), *Fable* (Xbox, PC, Mac), *Mass Effect* (Xbox, PC), *Alan Wake* (Xbox 360), *Fallout 3* (Xbox 360, PS3, PC), *Amnesia* (PC, Mac), *Super Meat Boy* (PC, Wii, Xbox 360, Mac), *Machinarium* (PC, Mac), *Cave Story* (PC, Mac) – also useful: videos of gameplay and strategy guides

Duration: Short starter, one lesson or extended project

Most computer games have a storyline where there is plot, protagonists and antagonists, and features often found in literature such as time shifts and flashbacks, character development and dialogue. Like film, games can provide an interesting source of material to study in order to understand storytelling.

There are a few ways this activity could be used:

a) For a shorter activity, pupils could watch the intro sequence to a game and analyse it to find out how the story is being told. Pupils could consider how they know where the story is set; who the main characters are and how they know that; what the conflict is, and the objective, in the story. For example, in the *Halo Reach* intro, how do the pupils know they are in space? How are the Spartan characters introduced. How do they learn about the team they are in and their first mission? What techniques are used to convey the beginning of this story and how does the end of the intro lead into the gameplay?

b) For a longer activity using a single game, pupils could watch the intro sequence and, perhaps, the first couple of levels played through, research videos of gameplay online and look at strategy guides. They could then decipher the narrative structure and explain what the story is and how it is told, describing the technical aspects of storytelling.

c) For a longer activity using several games, pupils could repeat (b) for three games and make comparisons between their stories and how they are told.

Extension: Intro sequences could be used as a beginning for a creative writing exercise. Most games have an intro sequence at the beginning and will either end on a cliffhanger or lead straight into the game. They will often provide an introduction to the environment, main characters and key conflict. Having watched the intro sequence, pupils could be asked to continue to write the story as a piece of prose or a script for a game or film.

Activity:	Literary References
Games:	*Dante's Inferno* (Xbox 360, PS3, PSP), *Limbo* (also links to *The Divine Comedy*) (Xbox Arcade), *Onimusha* (links to *Hamlet*) (Xbox, PS2, PC), *Lord of the Rings* Online (PC), *Call of Cthulhu* (based on the work of HP Lovecraft) (Xbox, PC)
Duration:	A short starter for a specific work or a whole lesson to analyse several and create own

There are a number of computer games which draw on literature for inspiration. This could be as direct as *Dante's Inferno* using the poem *The Divine Comedy* for inspiration, or *Onimusha* using names from *Hamlet* for its characters, including Fortinbras, Rosencrantz Guildenstern and Ophelia.

Pupils could analyse one or more computer games based on literature and speculate on why the developers have used these as inspiration. Also they could look at how they have been used, how true to the original they are and, if creative licence has been taken, how and why – and who is it for, the developer or the target audience?

For a longer activity, pupils could then discuss other works of literature which they think would make interesting games, and they could take one and develop it into a full idea. They should consider the genre, storyline and target audience for the game.

Activity:	Word Games
Games:	*Textropolis* (iPhone, iPad), *Fishtropolis* (iPhone, iPad), *Bookworm* (PC, iPhone, iPad, DS, Xbox Arcade), *Bonnie's Bookstore* (PC, Mac), *Typer Shark* (PC), *Word Harmony* (PC)
Duration:	Quick starters or plenaries

There are many casual games that are based on wordplay and these can be useful for developing vocabulary, improving spelling and generally working with words. As these games are often quite quick or can be played simply, when needed and for as long as needed, they can be quite a good way to start lessons, end lessons, or even be used as a reward.

The chosen game could be played together as a class, with the teacher putting it up on the board through a projector so all of the pupils can play together. Perhaps they could be split into two teams and work together to compete against their peers.

Played individually, the game could also be run as an activity in pupils' own time. Pupils who complete a level first or gain a high score (without cheating!) could get a reward.

Extension: Having played different word games, pupils could be asked to develop their own word game. They could include their own word lists, perhaps using words they find difficult to spell.

Activity:	Choose Your Own Adventure
Games:	Text adventures – short games like *9:05*, *Lost Pig And Place Under Ground*, and longer games like *Zork*
Duration:	20–30 minutes, one lesson or in own time

Choose Your Own Adventure books contained stories which were written in chunks and, at the end of each, the reader would be given options, such as: *Fight the spider, turn to page…*, *Run away from the spider, turn to page…* . Text adventure games (also known as **interactive fiction (IF)**) take this structure of story into game form.

Players are presented with a description of the scene and then can type in commands (such as *move west*, *open door*, *pick up lantern*). Players can move through the world, interact with objects (and sometimes other characters) and are usually required to solve puzzles in order to complete the game. The most interesting part of text adventure games is that there are no graphics – the game is played entirely through text. This means players must use their imagination to visualize the environment, characters and action in the story. Sometimes players need to draw their own maps on paper, as they move through the world and record where objects are and the pathways they take. This is definitely needed for big games like *Zork!*

Pupils in pairs could be asked to play a short text adventure game, such as *9:05*, and play through until the end. This should take about 20–30 minutes, depending on the pupils playing it. They could then be asked to carry out an analysis, such as looking back over the commands they put in, the way the story has been told, playing again to see if different options get a different result, or examining how characters or dialogue have been used.

These games are great for developing literacy skills and imagination, as they are just like reading books, except the reader gets to interact and control the action.

Extension: Having played at least one text adventure, pupils could be asked to create their own. There is great software available to help do this, such as *Adrift* (see page 74). Alternatively, they could create the book version of Choose Your Own Adventure.

Activity:	Game Advertising
Games:	None, although examples might be useful of *Dead Space 2* (video trailer), *Dead Island* (video trailer), *Deathtrap Dungeon* (print advert), *Spawn: The Eternal* (print advert), *Daikatana* (print advert)
Duration:	One or more lessons

It could be interesting to study advertisements for computer games when looking at persuasive writing. These could include billboard advertisements, features on websites, magazine adverts or blurbs on game boxes. All the features usually analysed for advertising can be found; however, there are two additional aspects which can make this investigation very interesting.

a) Audience: who is the advert targeting? If the game is rated 18, is it targeted at over 18s, under 18s, or parents? For younger rated games, are they written for children, their parents, or trying to attract a wider audience?

b) Controversy: are the manufacturers of the game trying to provoke it? Some games try to gain publicity based on something controversial; for example, the advert for *Dead Space 2* showed mothers watching the game and being shocked and horrified by it, the tagline being: *It's revolting, it's violent, it's everything you love in a game and your mom's going to hate it.* Alternatively, are the game makers going in the opposite direction and trying to justify why the games are beneficial, perhaps educational, giving reasons why they are 'not bad'?

Extension: Having looked at game adverts, pupils could be given a fictional game to advertise, with a particular rating and audience. They could be asked to design a billboardadvertisement, a full-page magazine advert and a box cover (front and back). You may wish to give your pupils a minimum word count for each, so they do not rely too heavily on imagery.

Activity: Machinima 1

Games: A game to use to create the machinima

Duration: Extended project, at least two lessons, but preferably more or to work on in own time

Machinima is the art of using game footage to create movies. See page 76 for more explanation on how to create machinima.

Pupils could be asked to use a game or several games to create a story or an advertisement for a product using machinima. They should be encouraged to design it first, compiling a script and considering details such as where in the game environment it should take place. They may also need to consider 'actors' for multiplayer and a voice-over.

Extension: As a longer project, such as for an extra-curricular activity, pupils could work in a group to develop a series of high-quality machinima films. They could aim to release one every fortnight or month, or perhaps a longer piece of work at the end of each term.

Activity: Game Review

Games: Game(s) to review

Duration: One lesson or a plenary with homework

Computer games can sometimes live or die by the reviews they receive, either in magazines or online. With a lot of reviews often being in one place, reviewers have only language (including a catchy headline) and perhaps a couple of images (usually screenshots from the game) to make their review stand out against the others and attract a reader to choose to read their review.

Pupils could look at existing reviews and then be asked to write their own. It would be useful for them to play the game they are reviewing. It is, however, best that this is a game they have not played before, so they have just an impression of it, as a reviewer would in the real world.

Extension: It has often been rumoured that game reviewers, more so in the 1980s and 1990s, have sometimes been persuaded by publishers to give a game a positive review even though they may not have thought it was good. Ask your pupils to write a review about a bad game (real or imagined) but put a positive spin on it. They will need to select their words carefully as they will not want to praise it too fully (and risk damaging their reputation too much) but cannot be negative (to please the publishers).

Activity:	Game Dialogue
Games:	Example game(s) *Mass Effect 3* (Xbox 360, PC), *Red Dead Redemption* (Xbox 360, PS3), *LA Noire* (Xbox 360, PS3, PC), *The Elder Scrolls IV: Oblivion* (Xbox 360, PS3, PC)
Duration:	One lesson or more

Most games use dialogue as a key part of telling their story. This will be spoken by the characters and is also sometimes displayed on the screen as subtitles. Also often accents, colloquialisms and other features of spoken speech are used as part of the script.

Pupils could be asked to watch the dialogue of an intro sequence or cut scene and analyse how speech is used. If there are different accents, colloquialisms or other unusual features of speech, the pupils could consider how this affects their enjoyment or understanding of the chosen game.

Extension: Pupils could be asked to write a script and record what they think might happen next in the story, using the same dialogue styles as the game.

Activity:	Journal of a Game Character
Games:	Examples such as Mario, one of *Pacman*'s ghosts, a Space Invader, Lara Croft, a puppy from *Nintendogs*, a bird or pig from *Angry Birds*
Duration:	Series of starters or plenaries, one lesson or homework

Games usually have well-defined characters which can make their stories deeper and playing more immersive. There are classic characters that have been around for a while, like Mario or Lara Croft, those that just appear in one game such as Faith (*Mirror's Edge*) and Frank West (*Dead Rising 1*), or the four very different characters alone in a world of zombies in *Left 4 Dead*.

Pupils should begin by watching cut scenes, playing and/or watching footage of a particular game. Then ask them to consider a specific character: perhaps the playable character, a NPC (who is not controlled by the character) or even the antagonist. They should think about the situation the character is in in the game but also their character's 'wider life'. Pupils should then write a journal with several entries describing their character's experience from a first-person perspective. They could be allowed to use creative licence for the parts of the game they have not yet seen and also for inventing what happens outside the game.

This activity could be set as homework attached to a lesson which has used a game in another way.

Geography

All computer games take place in an environment and, although many are fictional, there are some which are realistic and can be used to see real places without needing to travel there. They have been replicated so exactly that using them for study can be a fascinating experience. In addition, because all games use geographical environments, they can be an interesting basis for non-playing activities.

Activity: Flight Simulators

Games: *Microsoft Flight Simulator X* (PC)

Duration: One lesson or a series of starters or plenaries

Flight **simulators** often use real-world geography as their terrain. They allow players to fly across the landscape and in some, such as *Microsoft Flight Simulator X*, have a **free roaming** mode where players can fly anywhere in the world.

Pupils could be asked to form flight teams including a pilot, co-pilot and navigator. Each team could pick a destination out of the hat. First, they should identify it on a globe and then attempt to fly there in the aeroplane in the game. While one team is flying, the other teams could be tasked with listing all the things about that location that they can remember or researching online and creating a fact sheet.

This activity could form one lesson or work nicely as a starter or plenary for a set of lessons with each team taking a turn in the aeroplane.

This activity could also be suitable for Travel and Tourism as the whole class becomes people on the plane including passengers, flight attendants, etc. While the pilot is flying to the destination, the flight attendants could have to deal with difficult passengers, serve drinks and ensure everyone is safe and happy.

Extension: Driving simulators can also use realistic geography, such as *Test Drive Unlimited* (Xbox 360, PS2, PC, PSP) which accurately models the whole island of O'ahu and features over 1000 miles of roads and highways. Similar activities could be carried out using this game, perhaps as a taxi driver for Geography or a coach trip for Travel and Tourism.

Activity: Make a Race Map

Games: None

Duration: Short version – 10–20 minutes, long version – one lesson

Racing games often use real-world locations to form their race tracks. This activity uses that idea and asks pupils to create their own fictional race tracks using real-world geography. Pupils could be provided with street maps of a city or larger maps for races in mountains or desserts.

a) Short version: This could be used to introduce pupils to a place which they are shortly going to begin studying. They are asked to look at the map and quickly decide the route they would like their race to take. The aim is to get pupils to look at the place and have an idea of what it looks like. For this shorter version, you may wish to use quite a simple map for that area.

b) Long version: Pupils could be given real maps such as city A–Zs, OS maps and others which have a lot of detail. Their race tracks must take into account the notations on the map such as contour lines, the width of roads, bridges, emergency service access and other features. They should take into account the safety of the drivers, considering there will be several cars on the route at one time. Once they have created their tracks, they could swap with another pupil and check each other's to see if they can spot any potential problems.

Extension: To add more complexity, pupils could be challenged to include one hair-pin bend, a steep incline and/or make the race last for a certain distance or time.

Activity: Map-reading Skills

Games: Games where a physical map comes with the game e.g., *GTA IV* (Xbox 360, PS3, PC), *The Saboteur* (Xbox 360, PS3, PC), *The Elder Scrolls V: Skyrim* (Xbox 360, PS3, PC)

Duration: Quick activity for a starter or plenary

All large commercial games have maps in the game environment but some also come with physical maps in the box or you can print the maps from the internet. To practise map-reading skills and navigation, pupils could use them in quick activities to exercise these skills.

Pupils could be given a set of instructions and have to follow them to arrive at a secret location. Alternatively, pupils could be given a location on the map and be asked to work out the shortest/easiest/safest route to arrive there. These could be done as a competition where the first pupil to complete the route or reveal the secret location 'wins'. Alternatively, pairs of pupils could each be given different challenges and each time the activity is run, they are swapped around and given different ones.

Extension: Pupils could be asked to write instructions from one location to another and then swap with another pupil to see if they can follow them, and vice versa.

Activity: City Design

Games: None, unless examples wanted

Duration: One lesson or set for homework

Many computer games are set in cities, sometimes based on real ones and sometimes entirely fictional. However whether they are cities of the future or the past, well-designed ones generally have certain standard features such as roads, transport systems, government (or similar) buildings, residencies, public facilities and shops. Pupils could be first asked to make a list of all the features which must be in a city and those which would be desirable. Then they should design a futuristic city for a game including all of these features. They should create a map, descriptions of the city and describe the game which takes place in it.

Extension: This activity could be developed to include a visit to the nearest town or city and pupils could analyse what they see in real life, compare it with cities in games and then use this analysis in their own city designs.

History

Computer games often use history as a basis for their storylines, environments or characters. Whether this be modern history, such as the World Wars, medieval history, such as kings and queens, or old or ancient history, using Greek mythology or a Roman world.

Activity: World War II Experience

Games: *Call of Duty 2* (Xbox 360, PC, Mac), *Brothers in Arms* (Xbox 360, PS3, PC)

Duration: One lesson

Computer games can provide very realistic experiences and, unlike film, because they are interactive can immerse a player in the situation and make it feel even more real. Instead of using a film such as *Saving Private Ryan*, consider using a computer game. Games can be useful for subjects such as World War II for giving pupils a fuller idea of the realisms of war. Obviously, be careful in choosing the games; you will need something which has been modelled accurately on war (as with those suggested above), rather than those which include zombies or other unrealistic elements!

Pupils could take turns to play the game on the big screen, perhaps while others are watching or carrying out work (such as identifying elements of the game on the screen). Alternatively, you could ask someone who is good at the game to play it for the pupils to watch, and perhaps carry out work. Although this second method is not interactive for the pupils, it could be used for the first part of the game to get them going, and then pupils take over once they have had the core experience. This could be especially good for a game such as *Call of Duty 2*, as it has a similar start to *Saving Private Ryan* as the troops land on Normandy beach.

Activity: Vietnam Experience

Games: *Shell Shock: 'Nam 67* (PC), *Battlefield Bad Company 2: Vietnam* (Xbox 360, PS3, PC)

Duration: One lesson

Similar to the World War II Experience, there are some games which have used the Vietnam war as their basis and have realistically and accurately recreated the feeling of being part of that war.

Pupils could either take turns to play through the game or watch someone good play a part of it to give them an idea of what it was like to be in Vietnam at that time.

Activity: Snapshots of History

Games: *The Cat and the Coup* (PC indie), *Anno* series (1404, 1503, 1602, 1701) (PC)

Duration: One lesson or set for homework

Some games, often small indie games, take moments from history as their basis that are not the 'popular' ones such as the world wars or medieval conflicts. *The Cat and the Coup*, for example, describes itself as a 'documentary videogame' and details a coup against the first democratically elected Prime Minister of Iran, Dr Mohammed Mossadegh. The player takes the role of his cat and leads him through the key events of his life, solving small puzzles in order to unlock new parts of the story. The artwork is also fitting as it is in a Middle Eastern style.

Extension: *The Cat and the Coup* would be great paired up with the animated film *Persepolis* to learn more about life in Iran in the twentieth century.

Activity: Your Historical Game Version 1

Games: None

Duration: One lesson, ongoing side-project or set for homework

Many computer games are based on battles or wars. Fighting in games is interactive, competitive and can involve many aspects such as tactics, strategy and bravery. There are many games which use these as a basis, but there are numerous interesting battles from history which have not yet been the subject of a game.

Pupils (possibly in small groups) should select an interesting but somewhat obscure battle. This could be an invasion in Anglo-Saxon times, a medieval conflict in the War of the Roses, a clash between Roundheads and Cavaliers or a lesser known battle from the Crimean, Boer or World Wars. It could even be a modern war from the twenty-first century. Pupils should create the idea for a mini-game based on their chosen topic. They should decide the structure of the game (e.g., first-person shooter following a main character, **top-down strategy** playing a leader managing his armies, **role-playing game (RPG)** where the player plays a minor character who progresses to become a great leader). It would be hoped that once they have started this activity, pupils would get involved and enjoy it.

Extension: Once they have the structure in place, pupils could design the characters, environment and sketch what would appear on the screen. They should think about **HUD** elements, such as lives, health, mini-maps, and so on. Pupils should decide what important things the player will need to know, for example, the number of soldiers alive on the battlefield. They can be creative in this and go into as much detail as they wish.

Activity: Your Historical Game Version 2

Games: None

Duration: One lesson, ongoing side-project or set for homework

Many games are set in historically interesting locations but there are other locations which are more obscure and ripe for using in creating game ideas.

Pupils (possibly in groups) should choose an historical location, such as an historical building they might have been studying. For example, if they have been carrying out a project about Henry VIII, they could choose Windsor Palace, the Tower of London, Hatfield House, Westminster Abbey or Hever Castle. Once the location has been selected, pupils should create their characters and decide what form the game will take, such as a role-playing game (RPG), **platformer** or **point-and-click adventure**.

Activity: Mythology References

Games: Characters/games based on classical mythology, such as *Viking: Battle for Asgard* (Xbox 360, PS3), *God of War III* (PS3)

Duration: Starter for a specific work or a whole lesson to analyse several

There are a number of computer games which draw on classical mythology for inspiration, such as *God of War III*, which is based on Ancient Greek Mythology and sees Kratos and the Titans at war with Zeus and the gods on Mount Olympus.

Pupils could analyse one or more computer games based on mythology and speculate on why the developers have used these stories as inspiration. Pupils could look at how they have been used, how true to the original they are and, if creative licene has been taken, how and why – and who is it for, the developer or the target audience?

Extension: Pupils could discuss other works or areas of mythology (or from other cultures) which would make interesting bases for games, and they could take one and develop it into a full idea for a game. They should consider the genre, storyline and target audience.

Languages

Computer games use a huge amount of spoken, and written, language to convey the stories they are telling and as such provide a rich source of ideas for activities.

As well as those in this section, please also see the activities for Drama (pages 32–33) and English (pages 34–40).

Activity: Language Change

Games: Most games have an option to change the language (stated on the box)

Duration: Starter or 10–20 minutes

Most large-scale commercial computer games involve a lot of dialogue or narration and have options to change the language and add subtitles.

Pupils could be asked to watch an intro sequence or cut scene in a different language and asked to translate it and explain what is happening in the story.

Extension: Once pupils have done this activity, they could be asked to progress the story further by writing in prose or script what they think happens next and even acting it out or recording it.

Activity: Description of a Game

Games: Any game would be suitable, whether a small, casual game or something larger

Duration: A short starter or a longer activity

Pupils could be asked to play mini-games (perhaps individually on PCs) or watch a larger game being played for all of the class. Then ask them to describe the game in the desired language. They may need some genre-specific words, such as spaceship and alien or wizard and magic, depending on the type of game. For a short activity, you could ask pupils to focus on creating a general description. Alternatively, for a longer activity, ask pupils for more detail, including describing the characters, the environment, the story and how the game is played.

Their descriptions could become an extended piece of prose or be developed into an audio or video recording.

Extension: The description could be extended to become a review of the game, allowing pupils to not just be descriptive but also to convey their opinion.

Maths/Numeracy

Computer games sometimes use mathematical concepts in their gameplay, such as the player needing to employ calculating with numbers, working out angles or probability to have a better chance at something which appears random. As players are having fun, they may not even realize they are using their maths skills.

Activity: Gambling

Games: *Fable 2 Pub Games* (Xbox Arcade)

Duration: 30 minutes to one lesson

Fable 2 Pub Games is an extension of a bigger RPG called *Fable 2*. *The Pub Games* were part of the bigger game but were so popular, they were released as a standalone game. These games are interesting as the designers have taken existing games and changed them to introduce their own rules.

Gambling can be interesting to study as it involves factors such as probability, odds and ratios. Pupils could play the games and then be asked to analyse the rules. The activity could culminate in them working out the best way to win each game.

Extension: Once the pupils have had experience of the existing games, they could be asked to create their own 'pub game', taking into account fairness, fun and calculating the probability of winning or losing.

Activity: Angles and Trajectory

Games: *Angry Birds* (iPad, all Smartphones, PS3, PSP, PC, Mac)

Duration: A starter or plenary, or used throughout a whole lesson

Angry Birds has become a hugely popular game. Evil green pigs have stolen the birds' eggs and are hiding in various structures. Players control the birds which are launched from a slingshot, either aiming to hit the pigs directly or smash into the structures which can land on the pigs and eliminate them. There are different coloured birds, each of which has different properties (e.g., yellow can dash at high speed, black can drop bombs, and green can curve back like a boomerang). Players are given a limited number of certain birds for each level and must work out how to eliminate all of the pigs. This game would be good shown on a big screen to the whole class. By showing it on a whiteboard, you could load up the level then discuss with the class how best to approach the puzzle, drawing some of their ideas on the board. If used as a starter or plenary activity, one level could be done each lesson – although make sure the pupils are not late for the next lesson because of particularly tricky levels!

To extend this, pictures of different levels of *Angry Birds* could be used as questions for the pupils, asking them to work out the best way to complete the level and/or work out the measurements of the exact angles used.

This activity would be good for Physics as well.

Extension: Pupils could be asked to design their own levels for the *Angry Birds* game on paper. Designs could then be swapped within the class (or with another class studying the same topic) and pupils asked to work out the best way to complete the level with the birds given.

Activity:	Maths Games
Games:	*Puzzler Sudoku* (PC), *Sudoku Master* (DS), *Hands On Tangrams* (DS), *Super 7* (S), *Dr Kawashima* games (DS, Wii, Xbox Kinect)
Duration:	Short starters or plenaries

There are many casual games based on maths which can be great for short activities. Some are derived from traditional puzzles, such as Sudoku or tangrams. However, there are also games developers who have devised their own maths puzzles as the basis for the games, like *Super 7*.

For the activity, the game could be shown on a board for the whole class to take part in or pupils could be divided into pairs or small groups. Each time, the aim could be to complete a level or equivalent.

Extension: By asking pupils to create their own maths-based game, they must not only use their maths skills and show understanding and application but also consider how to make the game fun and challenging.

Media and Film Studies

Computer games are inextricably linked to Media and Film; however, these activities might suggest some uses for games which you may not have come across before.

Activity: Test Your Film Knowledge

Games: *Scene It?* series (Xbox 360)

Duration: About 30 minutes for a short game or 60 minutes for a long game

The *Scene It?* series of games began as DVD board games and has now been translated into a computer game series. The game can be bought with the four game remotes or separately if you already have them. Players are asked a series of questions about movies, which they sometimes take turns to answer and sometimes 'buzz in'. There are different categories, including answering questions about a movie clip and identifying a movie from the credits. The range of movies is quite wide and draws from all different genres.

Pupils could be asked to get into four teams and play against each other to find a winner. For each round, a different pupil could be in charge of the remote, so they all get a chance to buzz in and answer. It is quite a fast-paced game so there is not much time for discussion, but team members could help each other.

Extension: Pupils could be asked to create their own version by finding clips of movies online (or clipping them from an actual movie) and writing questions. They could also replicate other rounds such as *Who Am I?* (giving clues to an actor's identity), *Anagrams* or *Sound Clips* (where they pull a section of audio from a movie). Games could then be played using the pupils' own rounds and instead of buzzers, teams could shout to buzz in ('Red!', 'Blue!').

Activity: Genre

Games: *Red Dead Redemption* (Xbox 360, PS3), *LA Noire* (Xbox 360, PS3, PC), *Halo* series (Xbox, PC, Mac), *Left 4 Dead* (Xbox 360, PC, Mac)

Duration: Short demonstration or one lesson for a longer study

There are a number of games which have taken distinctive film genres and used them as a basis for their storylines, visuals and characters. These can be interesting for analysis alongside movies within that genre. For example *Red Dead Redemption* is very much in the Western tradition and *LA Noire* uses many traditional elements of 1940s film noir.

Pupils could watch the intro sequences and cut scenes and watch a good player work through some levels or missions. Alternatively, they could take turns to control the action on screen. While other pupils are watching, they could be asked to identify all of the elements that show it belongs to a certain genre or complete questions or worksheets based on what they are seeing on screen.

From this, there could develop a discussion about genre in general or about that particular genre, bringing in media references of movies and books.

Extension: Pupils could be asked to carry out research (perhaps as homework) to list as many games and movies in that genre as they can and for each give one distinct reason as to why they think it can be classified in that genre. You can decide whether crossovers are allowed.

Activity:	Machinima 2
Games:	A game to use to create the machinima or one with in-game machinima abilities like *Skate* (Xbox 360, PS3)
Duration:	Extended project, at least two lessons or more, or to work on in own time

Machinima is the art of using game footage to create movies. See page 76 for more explanation on how to create machinima.

Pupils could be asked to use machinima to create a trailer for a movie or game, real or fictional. As part of this they could be asked to storyboard it and write the script first. They could also be given restrictions such as a strict time limit, number of characters, and so on. To make it more realistic, you could give pupils a budget and starting costs, such as A-list actor = 20k, travel to a different country = 5k. Even though the pupils are using machinima to make the trailer, they could pretend they are using real people, locations and props and carrying out a real-world project.

There is also an activity using machinima in the English section (see page 38)

Extension: Other machinima projects could include making a promotional video for their school, explaining a concept (such as genre or binary opposition) or creating a mini comedy or game show.

Activity:	Film/Game Tie-Ins
Games:	*Kung Fu Panda* (Xbox 360, PS2, PS3, Wii, DS, PC), *King Kong* (Xbox 360, PS2, DS, PSP, PC), *Spiderman 3* (Xbox 360, PS2, PS3, Wii, DS, PSP, PC, Smartphones), *Cars 2* (Xbox 360, PS3, Wii, DS, PC, Mac), *The Godfather: The Game* (Xbox 360, PS2, PS3, Wii, PSP, Smartphones), *Lost: Via Domus* (Xbox 360, PS3, PC), the *Lego* series (various)

Duration: Short demonstration or one lesson for a longer study

It is quite rare now for a big-budget movie to be released without a computer game accompanying it. Even in the earlier days of computer games, in the 1980s, there were many games released based directly on movies.

Pupils could watch or play the game and consider questions such as how faithful it is to the movie, how the storylines compare, whether the characters develop in a similar way, whether the game is restrictive (e.g., whether it forces players to follow the events of the movie), whether the visuals are comparable, and if the game has the same mood and tone of the movie. There could also be a discussion about the limitations of movies versus games; for example, movies are more realistic because they use real actors, whereas games make the impossible happen (without costing a fortune in special effects!). There could even be an interesting debate on which medium is better. If pupils are not forthcoming in these discussions, you could allocate them a point of view and give them cards with 'hints' on to spur the conversation, especially for those who often do not get involved.

Extension: Pupils could take a movie which does not have a game tie-in and design one themselves. They would need to consider audience (and rating), type of game, characters and storyline. They should decide how closely the game will follow the movie plot and whether the game will be side-by-side with the movie or whether it will add something to it, perhaps following a side character's story or showing what happened before or after the movie. They will need to consider their USP. For people who have just paid to see the movie (either in the cinema or on DVD), what would persuade them to pay more money to buy the game?

Music

The music of computer games has changed from being blips of various tones played quickly together (like on *Nintendo GameBoy*) to full-scale orchestral pieces, some of which have won awards, and it is now becoming a discipline of its own like film soundtracks. There are also games which have music at the core of the concept and require players to use rhythm and tone skills.

Activity:	Rhythm Games
Games:	*Rock Band* (with 'instruments') (Xbox 360, PS2, PS3, Wii), *DJ Hero* (with 'decks') (Xbox 360, PS2, PS3, Wii), *Dance Central* (Xbox 360 Kinect), *Elite Beat Agents* (DS) *Boom Boom Rocket* (Xbox Arcade)
Duration:	Each game would likely take one lesson to include all pupils taking turns

There are several games which use music and rhythm as their foundation. Players need to use these skills in order to progress and, therefore, these improve as a result of playing the games. *Rock Band* allows players to play guitar, bass, keyboard, drums or sing vocals. *DJ Hero* uses a replica of decks for players to mix tracks using scratching and cross fades. These games require peripherals to be purchased as well as the games. *Dance Central* requires the player to move to the music, copying the moves of the dancer on screen – although this does not need a peripheral, it does need Kinect and plenty of room! Other rhythm games such as *Elite Beat Agents* or *Boom Boom Rocket* are played with the controller and require buttons to be pushed at the right time in the music.

Pupils could take turns, perhaps in groups, to play the games. For a more structured activity, *Rock Band* could be used and the class could be split into several 'bands' where each pupil has their own 'instrument'.

These games are likely to be popular with some pupils and you will need to be quite strict to make sure they stop when asked, to ensure everyone has a turn. Conversely, some pupils will not be keen to play. However, these are the pupils who are also unlikely to be keen to play any instrument or sing in Music and using games might be a way to encourage them to join in, especially if they are working in a team with their friends.

Extension: The bands could be set up, with names and characters, before the lesson, and during the lesson the bands could compete to gain the most fans, score the most points or collect the most stars.

Activity:	Analysing Game Music
Games:	*Left 4 Dead* (Xbox 360, PC, Mac), *Puzzle Quest: Challenge of the Warlords* (various), *Hitman 4: Blood Money (Ave Maria)* (Xbox 360, PS2, PC), *Halo* series (Xbox, PC, Mac), *The Legend of Zelda: Ocarina of Time* (Nintendo platforms only)
Duration:	One lesson

Music made for games is increasingly becoming a respected area and is beginning to be on a par with film soundtracks. In an article in *Joystiq* it was revealed that the Grammy

Awards were to be adjusted to allow computer game soundtracks to be equally valid to win an award as film and television in four categories.

Computer games need music to set the mood and create an atmosphere, whether it be fun and light-hearted or dark and threatening. Music can be used at crucial parts of the story, just like in a film. Analysis of these soundtracks can be very interesting and an area of investigation which your pupils may enjoy.

Other activities could include:

- Watching a game with the sound muted and discussing the experience.
- Listening to a piece of game music and guessing the type of game, when it might be used and what experience it is trying to convey.
- Comparing the music of games of different genres.

Extension: Pupils could be given a piece of game music, without being told what game it comes from (it doesn't really matter if they know it). They are required to either gather footage from the internet or record their own short movies to match the music. They could try to recreate a gaming experience, establish a mood or tell a story.

Activity: Game Without Graphics

Games: *In The Pit* (Xbox Arcade)

Duration: A starter for the whole class, or extended to last one lesson or more

In The Pit is an unusual game which is just based on sound and has no graphics. It requires surround sound to play or can be very effective using headphones. The player is a monster living in a pit under the control of an evil king and required to feed on the king's enemies who are thrown into the pit. In complete darkness, players must work out where the enemies are, using the surround sound noises and vibration feedback in the controller.

This game could be played as a starter involving the whole class. It would require at least four speakers to be set up – ask your IT Support for help with this and give them plenty of warning as they might need to rig up some extra equipment. Pupils could play the game together, with the teacher controlling and describing the sensation through the controller. The pupils will need to stay quiet, listen quietly then give advice to the teacher.

Alternatively, the game could be set up in a separate room with headphones. Pupils could go into the room one at a time to play for a set period (perhaps one level). While doing so, the rest of the class could be involved in another activity. The homework for all might be to write about their experience of the game.

Physical Education

Computer games are often criticized for creating couch-potato kids. However, in recent years games have become increasingly physical and can actually be a positive source of exercise. These activities either use games made for physical movement or encourage pupils to create their own exercises based on the games. These are great activities for a rainy day or those not keen on sport!

Activity: Get Active!

Games: *Wii Sports* (Wii), Wii Fit (with balance board) (Wii), Kinect Sports (Xbox Kinect), *Dance Central* (Xbox Kinect), *Fruit Ninja* (Xbox Arcade Kinect), *Kinect Adventure* (Xbox Kinect)

Duration: One lesson

There are many games now which require physical movement in order to play the game. It might be a simulated sport, dancing, or just moving to carry out tasks, avoid obstacles or karate chop fruit!

Pupils could take turns to play the chosen game or you could set up a tournament to find the champion. Alternatively use the games as part of a fitness circuit where pupils move from star jumps to shuttle runs and sit-ups. Use the multiplayer game of beach volleyball on *Kinect Sports*. These activities might take a little work in organizing, but could be really fun and encourage those not keen on sports to keep going as there is the 'reward' of playing a game as part of the workout.

Extension: Get the pupils involved in the planning of their activities and ask them to come up with ideas for activities using games. This might be a lesson just using one game, using several simultaneously, or as part of the circuit training. Being involved in the design of the exercising may make them even more enthusiastic to take part and work their hardest.

Activity:	Your Own Fitness Game
Games:	None
Duration:	One lesson or set for homework

Designing a game which involves movement can be difficult, especially as it is a relatively new area of games design.

Pupils could be asked to design a fitness game for Wii (with Wii Remote) or Kinect (no remote). They will need to decide on their target audience (someone keen on fitness or someone who needs persuasion), whether it will be an all-out fitness game or have the workout hidden behind fun activities, and what exactly players will do. Pupils should make it clear what parts of the player's body will be worked on by different parts of the game, how and why. They need to make sure the game is safe and will not cause harm to their target audience.

To develop this further, pupils could be asked to create sketches of the screen, act out players' movements and possibly even present the idea to the class. You could also take it one step further and put together a panel (perhaps including the Head of Sport or Head of ICT) and ask the pupils to pitch their idea (like *Dragons' Den*), with the panel giving feedback and choosing a 'winner'.

Extension: To give this activity an extra level of challenge, the pupils' games could have constraints such as: 'the technology will only detect the player's upper body', 'movements can only be on the x and y axis, but not diagonals', 'the target audience must be those who are disengaged in sport and this game must get them interested'.

Religious Studies

Many computer games overtly or subtly use religion as a basis for the characters or storyline. They may have characters or worlds where religion forms a part of life, perhaps as a source of comfort or a reason for conflict. Although some games do use real-world religions, very often they will not, in order to avoid offence or controversy. Instead, fictionalized versions are created, based on real beliefs and practices. At their core, most computer games are a struggle between good and evil, a concept also at the crux of religion.

Activity:	Which Path Will You Take?
Games:	Games where you can choose a good or bad path such as *Black and White* (PC, Mac), *Mass Effect* (Xbox, PC), *Star Wars: Knights of the Old Republic* (Xbox, PC, Mac), *Bioshock* series (Xbox 360, PS3, PC, Mac)
Duration:	Long project, possibly as homework or in own time

In most computer games players will take on the role of the hero, working for the side of good and righteousness. However, some games allow the player to make the choice whether they want to be good or evil. Either they will decide from the beginning which path they will take or events in the story will force players to choose.

Pupils could play one of the games suggested above and, once reaching a certain point in the game (or having played for a set time), they could be asked to write a report (or create a presentation or short video) explaining their experience. They should focus on which path they took, why and what were the consequences of that choice.

Extension: Pupils could play the game again and then say whether they made the same choices or not – and why.

Activity: Create Your Own Religious Game

Games: None

Duration: One or two lessons or set for homework

Makers of computer games will often avoid using religion overtly in their games. If they make the antagonist a certain religion, they could be accused of making a statement about that religion; similarly, if they are considered to be promoting a certain religion too much, the makers could be blamed for trying to brainwash young people. However, this still leaves a lot of scope for games with religious content.

Pupils could be asked to design a game involving religion. This could be using characters who follow religious traditions, storylines based on religious stories, or games to try and explain different aspects of a religion. They should consider their target audience, what message they are trying to convey and what type of game they will create (role-playing game, platformer, puzzle, point-and-click adventure). They could write an outline of the story, sketch the characters and screen design and describe the gameplay. As a final task (extending the project into a second lesson), pupils could be asked to put their ideas into a presentation which they can pitch to the class.

Extension: Religion in games can often cause controversy which can in turn have a positive or negative effect on the game. Controversy can cause the public not to buy the game or it can cause publicity and enhance sales, as people become curious about a game which causes such as furore. Ask pupils to comment on the potential controversy that could be caused by their peers' games and ask if this would create positive or negative attention.

Science

Computer games, as with other fictional media like films and books, have the opportunity to divert or ignore science, such as with the use of magic. However, most games have science at the root of the game mechanics, especially physics. In terms of educational activities, games which use real science can be helpful, but those which bend the rules of science are also useful, as pupils can identify where the changes have been made and the resultant effect.

Activity: Physics: Realistic Game Physics

Games: Games with realistic physics such as *Rockstar Table Tennis* (Xbox 360, Wii), *Half Life 2* (Xbox 360, PS3, PC), *Forza* series (Xbox 360)

Duration: One lesson

With advances in game technologies, computer games can have **increasingly realistic physics** where any action would have exactly the same response in real life, such as hitting a ball with a racket, that ball bouncing or the trajectory of a ball through the air when there is a breeze.

Pupils could get into groups and work round a set of different activities:

- Play a game with realistic physics, with their team mates making notes on the experience.
- Make a list of pros and cons of games with realistic physics.
- Discuss and list sports games which would benefit from realistic physics and why.

Extension: Having learned about games with realistic physics, ask your pupils (possibly in groups) to design a sports-based game which would use realistic physics. They can choose which sport they wish to use.

Activity: Physics: Unrealistic Game Physics

Games: Examples of games which use unrealistic physics, such as *Half Life 2* (Xbox 360, PS3, PC, Mac), *Portal 1* (Xbox 360, PS3, PC, Mac), *Portal 2* (Xbox 360, PS3, PC, Mac), *Boom Blox* (Wii)

Duration: One lesson

Although modern games can produce incredibly realistic physics, this also gives the opportunity to play with the rules. It may be that the majority of the games follow the rules of physics, for example gravity means the character has to stay on the ground, but they may break the rules or bend them, such as allowing for very high jumping or using portals to jump from one place to another.

Pupils could play one or more games with unrealistic physics and create lists of which rules are followed and which are not.

Extension: Having learned about games with unrealistic physics, ask your pupils to design a game, either individually or in a group. Discuss in advance what limitations, if any, to put in place for the games.

Activity: Physics: Universe Sandbox
Games: *Universe Sandbox* (PC indie)
Duration: 20–30 minutes, or longer if desired

Universe Sandbox is an 'interactive space simulator' which can be downloaded to try the basic tools and to buy the whole program is relatively cheap, whether buying singly or licence packs. Unlike other space simulators which often just show space as it is, this game allows players to experiment with the solar system. For example, players can move planets, introduce asteroids or add additional moons and suns. The program is highly accurate and can represent gravity precisely; so, for example, if a moon is added to an orbit around a planet and the gravitational pull of that planet is strong enough to affect that moon, it will spiral towards the planet and hit it. Rather than just looking at space – this allows pupils to learn through playing with it and changing it to see the effects.

I think the best way to use this program is mostly to let pupils play with it. Allow them ten minutes to explore the software and try whatever they want. Then give them a list of tasks to do, but keep them open (e.g., change the sun, add a meteor, change Saturn's rings). Ask pupils to make notes on what they did and what happened. Not only is this useful for their work, but if they do something interesting you might want to recreate it for the whole class to see.

Extension: Students could use their experimentation and learning from this game and create short animations or physical models of how the universe works, perhaps in teams with each group modelling a different aspect of cosmology.

Activity: Physics: Physics Puzzle

Games: *Crayon Physics Deluxe* (PC, Mac, iPhone, iPad)

Duration: A series of starters or plenaries

Crayon Physics Deluxe is a game where players can use crayons to draw on 'paper' and then the drawings become real objects in the game, with very real physics (e.g., gravity and momentum). There are puzzles to solve, some just as simple as moving a circle to a star. Players can choose how complex or easy to make it. Some of the puzzles can be solved very simply; but players can create a very convoluted system with their drawings to solve them. This is the sort of game which at first seems quite basic; but the more you use it, the more it develops and you can see the potential. I strongly recommend watching the video on their website (www.crayonphysics.com) or the videos on YouTube (especially those done by kids).

Pupils could be asked to solve a level as a starter or plenary on their own computers and the 'best' (quickest, most creative, most elaborate) solution gets to show it on the board in front of the whole class. Alternatively, you can show the level on the board and ask the pupils to come up with potential solutions, predicting what will happen when you add each drawing. With more than seventy levels, this can keep you and your pupils out of mischief for a while!

Extension: This can be taken further with students analysing the forces involved, the angles and effects of momentum, calculating accurately what they predict will happen then testing their theories.

Activity: Biology: Create Your Own World and Creatures

Games: *Spore* (PC, Mac, iPhone)

Duration: A series of starters, one or more lessons or an in own time

Spore is a game where players can create their own world. As stated on the website: 'It's a bit like the present you imagine a god might get on their first birthday: a mini universe of creation in a box.' It allows you to create all sorts of weird and wonderful creatures, develop their ecosystems, allow them to evolve and work up to creating tribes, civilisations and even space travel. Even though the creatures are of the player's design, it is a great way to demonstrate evolution. The great thing is, it is easy to use, entertaining and allows for a huge amount of creativity.

Pupils, perhaps in pairs, could begin their own ecosystem and create their own creatures and continue working on it to see it develop and grow. As they do so, they could keep a diary of progress which should show how their world is evolving and the creatures are changing.

Extension: At the end of the project, they could present their results to the class, including pictures of the creatures they created and excerpts of the diary they kept.

Activity: Biology: The Birds and the Bees

Games: *Viva Piñata* (Xbox 360, PC)

Duration: Ongoing project, possibly as homework

Viva Piñata is a game about maintaining a garden and attracting animals (*piñatas*) to it. The aim is to encourage rare and unusual *piñatas* to live in the garden by providing the right plants, features (such as water) and accommodation. Each *piñata* has its own diet and living needs. Once these are met and there are two of the same type of *piñata* living in the garden, then they can be bred to produce more *piñata*. Breeding is done very innocently with a 'romance dance'. *Piñatas* also have a food chain and they will fight with each other and eat each other.

Pupils could each be asked to create a garden and maintain it to try to encourage as many different *piñatas* as possible. A deadline could be set and the pupils with the rarest *piñata* or most well-kept garden could be the 'winner'.

Extension: Pupils could create a plan for their garden, either while they are playing or afterwards to say what they would have done next. This could include what plants they would grow, how they would breed their *piñatas* and costings using the in-game currency.

Technology Subjects

Although the term technology can relate to a variety of subjects, these are activities which could be used in different, related teaching areas. This could include ICT, Design and Technology or Food Technology.

Activity: Control

Equipment: Examples of game controllers

Duration: One lesson

There are many different types of game controllers available, associated with different platforms. PlayStation and Xbox have traditional dual analogue stick controllers; Xbox also has Kinect which requires no controller; Wii has the motion-controlled Wii Remote and PlayStation 3 has the PlayStation Move which will also receive motion commands. There are also unusual peripherals such as the guitars and drums for *Rock Band*, skateboard for *Tony Hawks Shred* and the Balance Board for *Wii Fit*.

Ask pupils to analyse the game controllers which are currently available. If they wish, they could also look at controllers that used to be available in the 1980s onwards and compare them with those available today. Then ask pupils to create a new controller. They do not have to worry about the platform with which it would be compatible. Instead, they should focus on the gaming experience, the practicality of the controller, how the game developers could make best use of it in their games, the safety of the product (e.g., flying out of hand into the TV screen!) and why it is different or better than those already available.

Extension: There are emerging technologies including virtual reality headsets and gloves. Ask your pupils to research these exciting new controllers, discuss whether they will become a reality for consumers and what the gaming experience might be with using them.

Activity: Food Technology
Games: *Cooking Mama* (DS, iPhone, iPad)
Duration: Starters or plenaries

In *Cooking Mama*, the player is given a recipe and asked to prepare the food. This could be as simple as boiled rice or as complex as spaghetti bolognese or beef curry. The recipes are real and the steps needed to prepare the food are accurate, except they have been turned into a game.

Cooking Mama could be shown on the screen through a projector to all the class and pupils could take turns to do each section of preparation. While doing so, you could discuss the real-world version of the techniques they are using.

Extension: Students could use the *Cooking Mama* recipes and attempt to make them in real life, perhaps adapting the recipes to add their own twist on the dish.

Skills Development

As well as being subject-specific, there are many uses for computer games which can develop particular skills. These are often those which are useful to pupils in their education and later life, but are sometimes difficult to pin down in the course of normal teaching. These activities might be suitable in teaching subjects where these skills are needed, as part of induction activities, in tutorials or end of term fun (which sneaks in learning without pupils particularly realizing).

In addition, these activities are great for pupils with SEN. It can provide development opportunities for those with needs; for example, improving their movement. Alternatively it can provide a more level playing field; for example, a pupil with dyslexia may struggle to gain average scores in class work but may do extremely well as a leader of a combat group, being able to strategize and verbally communicate with their team. Activities such as this can be great for self-esteem, making friends and changing opinions of their peers.

Teamwork

Teamwork is a hugely important skill for pupils to learn, as it is one which is asked for in almost every single job they may wish to apply for in the future. In addition, teamwork skills can help interpersonal relationships with peers, groups, socializing and even in relationships. Competences such as communication, compromise, strategy and negotiating are all integrated in this area. There is also an opportunity for identifying and developing leadership skills. You may find that the following activities encourage unlikely pupils to step forward to be the leader and excel. Hopefully this then becomes something on which you can continue to build, improving self-confidence and cohesion in the group.

Activity: Multiplayer and Co-op

Games: Examples include *Halo* (Xbox), *Ilo Milo* (Xbox Arcade), *At A Distance* (PC indie)

Duration: One lesson

There are many games which have multiplayer versions built in. A player can opt to play the story mode or alternatively play with others, either competitively or **co-operatively (co-op)**. By selecting a co-op, players may have to work in a pair or a team to solve a challenge, or there may be two teams working against each other to win by scoring more points.

The activity would need to be adapted, depending on which game was selected and how many people were taking part. Concentrate on encouraging the teamwork elements available in the selected game. For example, in *Ilo Milo*, two characters have to work together to solve puzzles. If you split the class into two teams, one team helping one player and one team helping the other, pupils will have to work together, communicate, share opinions, come to decisions as a group, to help the two characters on screen find the solution.

Activity: Create Your Own World

Games: *Minecraft* (PC indie)

Duration: Ongoing project

Minecraft is a game which can be run as a standalone played by one person; however, it is possible to set up a server and allow many players to meet in this online world and build projects together.

To set up a *Minecraft* server is straightforward. You need a computer with internet access and an account on *Minecraft*. You can download the server program from the *Minecraft* website and then install it. You can then go to the permission text file (saved with the files you have installed) and edit who is allowed to join your server. For more advanced permission tools you could install the *Bukkit* add on which would mean you had more control over the world and players on your server.

With a server set up, you could allow only your pupils onto your server and then set them challenges where they have to work together; for example, a large building project.

For other ideas, also see www.minecraftedu.com and www.minecraftteacher.net.

Motor Skills

With the increase of movement-based games, there is a great opportunity for using games to improve motor skills. Often these games either simulate real sports or require rhythm. The games encourage development in a safe environment, perhaps away from more able pupils, and allow a particular aspect to be practised again and again. Also they can be used solo, without requiring another pupil to play, for example a game like table tennis.

Activity: Rhythm

Games: *Rock Band* (with 'instruments') (Xbox 360, PS3, PS2, Wii)

Duration: One lesson

There are many rhythm games available which require players to move in time to music and with the action on the screen. Rock Band uses instrument **peripherals** to simulate actual instruments. For example, the standard guitar has five buttons on the fret board to represent pressing notes and a strum bar where the strings would be – the player has to press the right button and strum at the right time to 'hit' a note. There is a 'pro' version of this guitar which has a button for each place on the fret board, a different one for each string and each fret, and six simulated strings to strum, which is almost identical to playing a real guitar. It can be a great learning tool for that instrument.

Activity: Physical Movement

Games: *Wii Sports* (Wii), *Kinect Sports* (Xbox Kinect), *Kinect Adventures* (Xbox Kinect) *Dance Central* (Xbox Kinect)

Duration: One lesson or integrated with other activities

Although games are often thought to be sedentary, in recent years more and more movement games have become available. There are games such as the *Wii Sports* and *Kinect Sports* series which directly emulate real-world sports, but allow players to do them in the comfort of their own home (or school, in this case). Players are motivated by scoring points or beating high scores and can turn the difficulty up or down depending on the level of challenge needed. Games such as *Kinect Adventures* encourage full body movement but in the form of a game so the player often does not realize how much physical exercise they are doing.

    Kinect Dance Central recognizes players' movements for their whole body, including arms, legs, hips and head. Players can learn the moves one by one then recreate them for a whole song, making the right moves at the right time.

Activity: Hand–Eye Coordination

Games: *Geometry Wars* (Xbox 360, PC, DS), *Zen Bound* (PC, Mac, iPhone, iPad), *Tetris* (various)

Duration: Starters or plenaries

Video games are great for developing good hand–eye coordination and quick reflexes. Also they can develop pattern recognition, such as in *Tetris* where there are a limited number of shapes and, by learning those shapes, the brain can work out where they will fit with increasing speed.

    These types of games are good for anyone, young or old, but might be particularly useful with younger pupils who are developing their coordination still or those with special needs. In addition, used as a plenary they could be a 'treat' for good work during the lesson with the added bonus of developing dexterity as well.

Problem-solving

Problem-solving is a useful skill for all pupils and, once developed, can be adapted into different situations. For example, a pupil may never need to know how to cross a dangerous ravine by moving boxes into a logical pattern in real life, but probably will need to use spatial awareness, forward planning and judgment to play and enjoy sporting activities, navigate a new place of work confidently or even drive a car!

Activity: Games with Puzzles

Games: *Tomb Raider* series (Xbox, PlayStation, PC), *Half Life 2* (Xbox 360, PS3, PC, Mac), *The Secret of Monkey Island* (PC, Mac, Xbox Arcade, PlayStation Network, iPhone, iPad), *Portal 1* (Xbox 360, PS3, PC, Mac), *Portal 2* (Xbox 360, PS3, PC, Mac), *Chime* (Xbox Arcade, PlayStation Network, PC), *Minesweeper* (PC), *Lemmings* (PC), *Professor Layton* series (DS), *Dr Kawashima* series (Wii, DS)

Duration: Regular starter or occasional activity

Games with puzzles are great for waking up minds, getting pupils settled and interested at the beginning of a lesson. Alternatively, a longer session could be used several lessons apart but lasting for perhaps 20 minutes, for example to allow time for a level to be completed.

Pupils could play individually or the game could be played as a class. Each time it is played, the teacher nominates different people to be the player who controls the game and decider. The decider listens to all of the suggestions from the other pupils as to how to solve the puzzle and chooses which option the player should take – this can prevent it from becoming a free for all with ideas. The player has to wait for the decider to tell them what to do and must follow the instructions. Thus, pupils are also having to work as a team.

Strategy and Planning

Other skills which are useful in all walks of life are strategy and planning, the ability to organize resources, think ahead and see potential consequences and pitfalls – and avoid them. A number of games require players to manage their resources carefully. There may be only a limited supply of health, potions or other objects; some weapons or spells need to be used carefully because they take time to recharge before being able to be used again. Other games require players to find all of their items and, once used, it may need some effort to replace them.

Typing Skills

It is expected that all pupils will develop typing skills, especially by the time they have left school and have moved onto university or employment. For the most part this will happen naturally over time; however, as with most skills, practice makes perfect and there is no harm in helping the development of this very important skill by making learning fun.

Activity: Improving Typing Skills

Games: *Typershark* (PC), *Typing of the Dead* (PC)

Duration: Regular starter or plenary, or encouraged to play in their own time

It is important for all pupils to be able to type quickly and accurately. However, generally they no longer have lessons to learn this skill which will be used throughout their education, working life and even their social life. Therefore, giving pupils a regular activity to play a game which happens to develop this skill can be of real benefit. The activity could be done as a starter or plenary, perhaps not every lesson but once a week or once a fortnight. Alternatively, pupils could be encouraged to play the game in their free time, maybe with a chart of high scores in the classroom to encourage them to tell you how well they are doing and have a little bit of competition to improve.

General Knowledge

A common criticism I hear about pupils of all ages is that they lack general knowledge. This could be current affairs, vocabulary, world geography or history, politics, or even just general trivia or 'common knowledge'. Games can be a great, fun way to help pupils bolster this learning – and also, as with *Free Rice*, help charities at the same time!

Activity: Answer Questions – and Save the World

Games: *Free Rice* (PC indie)

Duration: Starter, plenary or activity in their own time

Not only is this game a good quiz, testing players on their knowledge of words and definitions, but it also helps charity. For every question answered correctly, the United Nations will donate ten grains of rice to the World Food Programme. Pupils can see the count rising as they answer questions correctly and are often spurred on by knowing they are doing good while playing.

Activity:	Who Wants to Be a Millionaire
Games:	*Who Wants to Be a Millionaire* (various)
Duration:	A quick starter or plenary, or a longer session of one lesson

The TV quiz programme *Who Wants to Be a Millionaire* is popular all around the world and the format should be known by your pupils. The questions set are all general knowledge and become increasingly difficult as the game progresses.

For pupils, you could use this as a starter or plenary by taking turns each week for a pupil to be in the hot seat, answering questions. You could keep a chart of scores and see who scores the highest once everyone has had a go. Alternatively, pupils could be playing for house points (or similar) or a small chocolate coin or another reward each time they play, the amount they get depending on how many questions they answer correctly.

Extension: A possible extension of this is to make your own version, and this could be subject-specific. Fancy graphics are not needed, although if you ask your IT department, they might be able to put something together for you. You need a set of questions for each amount of 'money', and the three life lines: for *ask a friend*, they could ask another pupil; for *ask the audience*, you could do a quick hands-up poll, and for *50:50*, you choose which two answers to take away.

More Exciting Activities Using Games

Geocaching

Geocaching (pronounced *geo-cash-ing*) is a relatively new activity and has come about with the improvement in GPS coverage and the reduction in price of the devices which use it. It is essentially treasure hunting where something is hidden, the coordinates are given and the cacher uses a GPS device (or SmartPhone) to locate it. It involves being outside (and has on occasion been nicknamed 'rambling for nerds') but in a school context could be restricted just to the school campus.

There are different types of clues which can be given. For a normal cache, the cacher will just be given the coordinates, although once at the location there often needs to be quite a bit of searching to find the actual object. A puzzle cache requires the cacher to solve a puzzle in order to obtain the coordinates, usually before they begin to search. A multi-cache is a series of linked caches where the first one gives the coordinates of the next and so on until the final cache is found.

The caches themselves are generally various types of waterproof boxes (such as Tupperware). In geocaching they will contain a log book, which is signed and dated by all the cachers who find it and valueless random objects. The principal is that the cacher finds the cache, signs the log, takes an object and replaces it with their own. In an educational setting, this can be adapted to suit the purpose of the activity.

Activity: Geocaching

Equipment: A cache (often Tupperware with something in it), a GPS or SmartPhone

Duration: One lesson

Before the lesson, hide a cache and take a reading of the coordinates. In the lesson, give the coordinates to the pupils and ask them to find the cache using their GPS or SmartPhone.

This could be done by sending one pair or team of pupils out at a time, asking them to sign the log and then re-hide it in the same place. The cache could contain some information about the topic they are studying, a clue to the homework they will be given or anything else which enhances the teaching of the subject. It could be a really fun way to spice up a dry topic.

This activity could also be used on a school trip; but make sure you always gain the permission of the property owner, any security are informed of what the boxes are and what your pupils will be doing, and that you have plenty of time to set it up.

Extension 1: A puzzle cache is one where a puzzle has to be solved in order to work out the coordinates of the cache. For example, the cacher could be told that the cache is at the coordinates North 51° AB.CDE West 001° VW.XYZ. The cacher needs to solve a puzzle in order to work out the values A–E and V–Z. Once they have worked it out, they can then find the cache – but only if they have worked it out correctly! Perhaps they need to use data about the topic they are studying, some maths or count certain items in their environment (e.g., number of green fence posts).

Extension 2: A multi-cache is where one cache leads to another. For example, the pupils are given the coordinates to the first cache and inside that are the coordinates to the next and so on, until they reach the final cache. Puzzle caches and multi-caches can be combined, so when the pupils reach each box they collect a clue and when it is all put together they can work out the coordinates to the final cache.

There is much more to geocaching, including *travel bugs*, *earth caches*, *whereigos* and *CITO* (cache in trash out). If you are interested in finding out more, visit www.geocaching.com and www.groundspeak.com.

Dragons' Den Pitch

In the television show *Dragons' Den*, budding entrepreneurs pitch their product and business ideas to five 'dragons' who might invest in their business. This can be replicated in an educational activity which can really challenge pupils in an exciting way and you are likely to see results you never imagined!

   Computer games are often pitched in this way, with the person with the idea presenting it to a panel who will decide whether it will go on to be developed. Another way games are pitched is the classic 'elevator pitch' where the person with the idea has to explain it quickly and succinctly, as though in a lift with a studio executive, and needs to convince them of the idea's merits before they get out of the lift.

Activity: Dragons' Den Pitch

Duration: At least two lessons or more

Ask pupils to come up with an idea. This depends on what subject and topic they are studying. For example, for an ICT lesson, this could be an idea for a new computer game; for Business Studies, it could be a business idea like in *Dragons' Den*. However for other subjects you could be more creative; for example, it could be a pitch for a new book or a documentary film on the topic, or a new invention which would improve the topic (e.g., in Geography or Science, a new 'green' technology).

   Once they have come up with their idea, pupils should put together a presentation which they will pitch to a panel. They should be given a date and time for their presentation, be told to dress smartly and be well prepared. You may want to give extra constraints such as they must bring in a prop or they can only use a limited number of PowerPoint slides. If you want the pupils to work in teams, explain that everyone in the team must be involved in delivering the presentation. Pupils should be encouraged to research, practice and refine, and be given enough time to do so, although you can expect that they continue to work on the project in their own time. Encourage pupils to consider this activity as real, and really 'lay it on thick' as to how important it is, perhaps suggesting that there will be rewards for those who do well and severe punishments for those who are late or unprepared!

   On the day(s) of the presentation, gather a panel of 'experts'. These could be colleagues who have a little spare time to give. Try asking teachers, support staff, teaching assistants, cleaning staff, admin staff and anyone else in the school who might be willing to help and who can give an interesting point of view on the pupils' ideas (perhaps a different perspective than a teacher, or someone who doesn't know the pupils).

   Invite each pupil (or team) to enter the room, stand in front of the panel and deliver the pitch. Then the panel has the opportunity to ask questions. Once happy, the panel can dismiss the pupil (or team). The panel should make notes during each presentation and you might want to use a standard form, with tick boxes for ease of use. The feedback should cover the idea being pitched and also the quality of the presentation including creativity, smartness and professionalism.

It is vital that, after all of the presentations have been delivered, perhaps in the next lesson, the pupils receive feedback. It is not just important to do the task, but for pupils to learn from the experience as well.

Extension: Before your pupils give their full presentation (at least one lesson before), ask them to do an elevator pitch. This should be 30 seconds to two minutes. If the idea cannot be summarized clearly and succinctly in that time, then there may be a fundamental flaw with their idea. This gives them an opportunity to return to the idea for improvement before the actual presentation.

Every time I have run this type of project, I have always been pleasantly surprised how much the pupils have enjoyed it, the amount of effort they have put in and how excellent their presentations are – and how smart they can look!

Points System

This is the modern version of gold stars. Gold stars are a little out-dated and can be seen as very babyish by pupils. Try these ideas which use the same principal but a more modern way of visualising it – it works in any subject.

Version 1: XP

In computer games, characters often earn XP (experience) to progress through the game – this idea allows your pupils to gain or lose XP through their work and behaviour.

- Put a wide horizontal bar (just made on paper) up on your wall (or alternatively this could be vertical perhaps made in a Blue Peter style from toilet-roll cardboard cylinders).
- Take a portrait photograph of each pupil and print it out.
- Start all pupils at 50 per cent XP (or alternatively an induction or introduction task could determine how much XP they start with).*

- Each time they do a good piece of work, demonstrate learning or do something which would earn them a gold star, award them XP and allow them to move their portrait up the bar.
- Similarly, for bad behaviour or poor work, they lose XP and have to move their portrait down.
- You may wish to award prizes for the pupil(s) with the most XP by the end of a term or project.

* Pupils should not start at 0 XP as a) if they lose some straight away, you have the problem of being in negatives, b) all pupils bring something with them and do not start with nothing and it demonstrates you are acknowledging that they are not empty shells, but do have some skills and basic subject knowledge

Version 2: Posse

This version is based on 'friends' – like those made in games or on social networking. The aim is to create a big posse by doing good work, helpful behaviour, and so on. Just like in classic Westerns, your pupils can create a posse through their positive actions.

- Again you need printed photographs of your pupils' portraits which they should put up on the wall.
- As they do something which deserves a reward, they are allowed to add a person to their 'posse' – they can do this by sticking a picture of someone beside their photo (e.g., a friend in class, member of their family or celebrity). When they have ten people in their posse, they can claim a bigger reward and then they start again. Alternatively, you could keep score of how many posses they create over a term and give a reward at the end.

Hero/Villain Design

A nice little activity is asking your pupils to design a new hero or villain, using those in computer games (or film or comic books) as inspiration. You could ask them to sketch them and then around it write their hero's/villain's name and what special powers they have. You could ask pupils to justify why their hero/villain exists (e.g., what they do that is useful or not been seen before).

This can be a good introduction lesson, perhaps when meeting a class for the first time, as whatever pupils create will likely tell you something about them and demonstrate their level of creativity and attention to detail. Alternatively, it could be an activity to 'pull out of the bag' when needed; for example, when you have unexpected cover or there is a power cut.

To extend this, you could put their heroes/villains on the wall (tell them you are doing this before they start) and then refer to them in your teaching. Perhaps it can be the basis for a points system in your class: for every piece of excellent work, their hero/villain can gain an extra power or item. For really good work or for the end of term, they could create a sidekick, pet or nemesis for their hero or villain.

Brainstorm Ideas for a Serious Game Teaching Core Concepts of a Subject

If there is a dry topic in your subject – and, let's admit it, there's at least one in every subject – you could ask your pupils to devise a new game for it. A good way to spark creativity and discussion about their proposed game is to put them into small mixed groups (not friendship groups) and give them large pieces of paper and several marker pens.

Give pupils five minutes to write down as many ideas for games as possible on one side of the paper. They could say types of games, characters from games, new ideas, things they would like to have seen in games, the types of games they would like to play for learning – anything they can think of. Push them for time, giving them minute warnings and counting down 30 seconds, 20, 10, 5, 4, 3, 2, 1.

Then tell them the topic which their game must teach the learner about. In their groups they should discuss all of the ideas they have written down and see if any can be combined to produce a game about the topic. Give the groups ten minutes to work on a fresh idea for a new game, circling the ones they are going to include.

For the rest of the lesson, ask them to use the back of the paper (or a separate sheet if preferred) and write out their idea for the game in as much detail as possible. They could give it a title, explain how it works and sketch their characters and the environment. Refer back to the list of game elements in the introduction on page 6.

The groups could present their ideas at the end of the lesson, or work on them for homework and present them the following lesson. Alternatively, they could be used as a basis for creating the actual games – see the next chapter for how to make your own games!

4 Making Your Own Games

It is possible to create your own games. I know that may sound difficult or time-consuming, but there are many tools available that have made it much easier than you might think. You do not need to know how to program to create games – you just need the ideas and the willingness to try.

Making your own games can mean you have tailor-made educational content which you can deliver using your unique, interesting, and fun game. You can also include specific things like the name of the school and even name the characters after pupils in your class (although be careful with this!). Your own game means you have full control over what happens, what is learned and you will know everything that can happen in the game.

Alternatively, you could carry out a project where your pupils make their own games. Again, you can specify the topic they cover and then give them the tools and freedom to be creative. Not only will they be learning about the topic as they make the game, but also continuing to learn about it as they play each other's. Pupils could brainstorm for ideas for the game (see page 72 for the activity *Brainstorm Ideas for a Serious Game Teaching Core Concepts of a Subject*) and then create it, either as an in-class project or as an ongoing homework project. Make sure you give your pupils enough time to complete the project, although not too long as they may need spurring along. Perhaps if you give them two deadlines, the first where they need to show the progress they have made and the second for the completed game.

All games that are made, whether by you or your pupils, can be used in other classes and even classes in the future as they reach that topic.

If you feel unsure about this but are keen to give it a go, ask your IT Support or ICT teaching department for advice.

Ways to Make Games

There are many different types of games you can make, from simple quizzes to more complex games using worlds and characters from big, commercial games. On the next page is a table describing some of the software available. For more information and hyperlinks to each, please visit www.karen-anderson.org Also you may have features on your own school's VLE to create games – ask your ICT Co-ordinator or IT Support team for advice. There are also games which can be used for developing levels within their game environments such as *Quake* and *Far Cry*, which are worth investigating if you are interested in developing further.

Using Computer Games Across the Curriculum

Software	Difficulty	Cost	Platform	Use	Website
Adrift	Easy to use	FREE (donations welcome)	Windows PC, Linux	Creates text adventures	www.adrift.co
Hot Potatoes	Easy to use	FREE	Windows PC	Creates interactive crosswords, anagrams and other word games	www.halfbakedsoftware.com
Quiz Creator	Easy to use	Free version online

Installed version $99/ yr (~£60) academic licence | Windows PC, Mac | Creates interactive quizzes | www.quiz-creator.com |
Sploder	Easy to use	FREE	Windows PC, Mac	Make platform, shooter, physics puzzles or top-down puzzle games	www.sploder.com/free-game-creator.php
Little Big Planet 1 or 2	Once pupils have basics, easy to use – tutorials available	Comes with game	PS3	Make your own levels within the *Little Big Planet* world	www.littlebigplanet.com/en/ game_guide/ps3/creating/
Halo Forge	Can be tricky to learn, but pupils who put in effort are rewarded – tutorials available	Comes with games, *Halo* 3 onwards	Xbox 360	Make your own levels within the *Halo* world	www.forgehub.com/

3D *Gamemaker*	Easy to use	£20	Windows PC	Creates simple games using a selection of pre-made assets (environments, characters, etc)	www.thegamecreators. com/?m=view_product&id=2126
Scratch	Uses basic programming but once pupils have the basics, they learn very quickly	FREE	Windows PC, Mac, Linux	Creates 2D animations, games, programs	scratch.mit.edu/
Kudo	User friendly, using basic programming concepts visually – tutorials and example projects available	FREE	Windows PC (uses controller rather than keyboard)	Creates mini-games in colourful *Kudo* environment	fuse.microsoft.com/page/kodu

Machinima

Machinima is the practice of making movies using game footage. It could be to tell stories, make comedy or give information. It can be an interesting type of assessment for vocational courses in any subject.

You can use open world games series such as *Halo*, *Grand Theft Auto*, *Fallout*, *Red Dead Redemption*, *Skyrim*, *World of Warcraft* – any game where you can walk around the world and act out the machinima script. To record the footage, you could use software such as *Fraps* which runs on a computer and captures audio and visual data that occurs during recording, which means it will capture the action on screen and the sound recorded through a microphone. For a console, a piece of hardware can be used to record the footage, as an extra device connected to it. The footage recorded can then be edited and added to, using ordinary video-editing software such as Microsoft MovieMaker (which is free with Windows PCs) or more advanced software such as Adobe Premier or Sony Vegas.

In-depth Game-making

For any pupils who are interested in taking game making further or have shown a talent for it, please refer them to your Head of ICT.

There are two main areas of skills which they could be encouraged to develop: design and programming, reflecting the core elements of game design. However other skills are important including creativity, storytelling, teamwork, communication and ideas generation.

Please see the last chapter of this book (page 83) for advice to give pupils who are interested in taking games development further and even considering a career in it.

5 Controversy in Games

Computer games are often surrounded by controversy. Violence, addiction, social isolation are all topics which orbit games and sometimes collide causing distressing headlines in the media. As teachers and tutors we can use these topics in order to create discussion and debate, and also introduce contentious issues to provoke thought, reflection and perhaps the forming of opinions.

Although games often come under heavy fire for issues of morality and social impact (admittedly sometimes rightly so), there are also a lot of positives about games which are often overlooked. Games can promote the development of skills which can be used throughout the player's life, such as dexterity, decision-making and strategy. Although the controversial topics are 'juicier' (page 81), please also take an interest in the positive aspects to gaming (page 81).

A Very Brief Introduction to Controversy in Computer Games

One of the first games to cause widespread controversy was *Death Race* (1976). It was a cabinet arcade machine and the display was black and white, but it was the content that created a stir. The player controlled a car on screen with a steering wheel and acceleration pedal. The aim was to run down as many 'gremlins' as possible. Although the graphics were crude, the 'gremlins' resembled stick men and the working title of the game had been *Pedestrian*, although Exidy, the game's creators, denied the intention was to promote violence. *Death Race* was the trigger for the first ever public protests due to a computer game.

Following this and, interestingly in a similar vein, *Carmageddon* (1997) was the first computer game to be censored in the UK and was also censored or banned in many other countries. The player races their car against other AI vehicles; however, bonus points and time could be gained for crashing other cars or running over cows or pedestrians. The publishers, SCi, wanted to get more publicity by submitting the game to be rated by the BBFC to obtain an 18, even though this was not a requirement before it was published. This back-fired as the BBFC refused to certify it. After ten months of appeal, the game as finally released with an 18 rating, but the blood had been turned green.

There have been other games before and since which have been changed owing to censorship or banned completely in various countries. In the United Kingdom, where the game rating laws are a bit quirky due to an alleged error in 1980s legislation and are currently under review, there have only been three games banned: *Carmageddon*, *Manhunt 2* and *The Punisher*, all three of which were released with 18 ratings once the offending material had been changed.

Admittedly some games are created or advertised in a certain way to cause more hullabaloo and therefore generate more hype and publicity. The game *BMX XXX* released in 2002 is an excellent example of this. Originally it was to be sponsored by Dave Mirra, a successful, medal-winning BMX athlete and focus on the sport aspect of BMX riding and stunts. However, the final game included crude humour and naked women, allegedly to spice up a lacklustre game. Mirra refused to have his name included in the title and took Acclaim, the publishers of the game, to court for damage to his image. The game garnered a huge amount of publicity, but it turned out to back-fire as shops refused to stock it. Sometimes this controversy would have been enough to pique people's interest and make it an underground hit. In this instance the game faded into obscurity, and somewhat into legend, as once gamers and critics made it past the contentious content, they reported that there wasn't actually a good game underneath.

Some games cause controversy by accident. *Portal 2* (2011), a puzzle game from Valve, came under fire for one line of dialogue in a huge script when one character mocked another for being an orphan. A father of an adopted daughter complained and it was blown up into a surprisingly large feature in the news. *Little Big Planet* (2008) had its release date delayed when it was discovered that one of the music tracks they had licensed for the game contained lines from the Quran. Sony decided to postpone the release, remove the song and repress the disks before putting it on sale. *Resistance: Fall of Man* (2007) stirred up criticism when leaders of the Church of England said a cathedral in the game looked very similar to Manchester Cathedral and declared it to be desecration and copyright infringement. Sony backed up the developers, Insomniac Games, and stated that it was set in a fictional environment and they had not intended to replicate the cathedral. The story hit national news and even the Prime Minister at the time was questioned about the issue. It was found that there was no merit in the copyright infringement claim and Sony offered the Church of England an apology. The controversy caused sales to rise and the game re-entered the top forty. Somewhat ironically, it is reported that the number of visitors to the cathedral also rose.

Suggested Lesson Plan

The following lesson plan could be used in a tutorial, for PSHE, Citizenship or equivalent subjects, or as an interesting discussion lesson at the end of term to provoke debate and opinions. The lesson plan is based on the topic of race in computer games, but any of the topics listed below could easily be slotted into this plan.

Lesson Plan

Aim: To introduce the topic of race in computer games and encourage discussion

Outcomes: By the end of the lesson, all pupils should have a grasp of the positive and negatives aspects of this issue and the key arguments. Most pupils will be able to explain the main points with examples and some pupils will have expanded the issue beyond the discussion of computer games and see how it relates to the wider world.

Resources needed:

Paper and pens for pupils to make notes; computers for pupils (working in pairs); teacher computer, project and screen

Approx. Timing	Teacher activity	Learner activity	Resources
5 mins	Welcome class Take register	Enter class and settle ready for lesson	
10 mins	Introduce the topic	Watch trailer for *Grand Theft Auto 4* Discuss the characters seen. What do they think of the main character? Is there any stereotyping? Why do we assume certain things about him? What are the developed wanting us to think?	Trailer for *GTA 4* Computer, projector, screen
15 mins	Arrange pupils into pairs Set task, then monitor their research, encouraging and supporting	Task: research online to find two more examples of games which use racial stereotypes. Ask them to look at articles or view movie clips from games – they should be encouraged to scan and, if the info they want isn't there, to move on quickly For differentiation give suggestions including try typing in 'videogames racial stereotypes' or looking up Cole Train from *Gears of War*, Lo Wang in *Shadow Warrior* or the racial gangs in *Grand Theft Auto* and *Saint's Row*	Computers for pupils in pairs Pens and papers to make notes

Approx. Timing	Teacher activity	Learner activity	Resources
15 mins	Bring class back together Describe how the lead playable character, CJ, in *Grand Theft Auto*: San Andreas was black; however, a mod was developed by a gamer and spread via the internet to allow players to put a 'skin' on him to make him look white. (more info available on website) Pose the question: why are the majority of playable human characters in games white?	Each pair briefs class on what they found Discuss what they thing about this. This could include whether they think the mod should be banned (if so, how and by whom?) and if *GTA* is the right game to have a black lead character (considering it is based around gangs and crime). Discuss their thoughts on this. This could include talking about the developers who make the games and the target audience who they want to buy the games.	You may wish to show an image of the character on projector/screen
10 mins (optional)	Teacher talks pupils through the stages of this task, supporting and asking questions about the final result	Pupils (in their pairs) return to the computers. They find a picture of a white game character on the internet and open it in Adobe Photoshop. Use the tools to change just the skin colour of the character's face. What effect does that have on the character? Would they be judged differently? Would players have reacted differently to the game?	Computers for pupils in pairs You may want support from ICT for this task – it is worth the effort. (instructions available on website)
5 mins	Plenary: Summarize topics discussed in this lesson (Optional) homework: choose one of the games, characters or issues discussed in this lesson and create a two-minute video or presentation explaining a point of view or two sides of an argument.		

See www.karen-anderson.org for more information on these topics and other controversies in computer games.

Note: As with any research on the internet there is always a chance that pupils will come across negative imagery or bad language. This is especially so when researching games rated Mature, which they may do in this lesson. It is worth giving a small warning before they use the computers and ask that they act maturely and, if they do encounter something unsavoury, just move onto a different page or video.

Negative Topics

Although there are many negatives associated with computer games, this gives teachers an opportunity to discuss interesting, controversial and valuable topics, using references that pupils will either know or easily identify with. By using issues in games as a starting point, more sources and examples can be brought in and the discussion can grow.

In addition, a lot of these topics are ones which pupils will be likely to have an opinion on or care about and will want to be involved and voice their opinion. This could encourage those who do not often contribute to engage.

These topics include:

- gender and sex
- race
- values: violence, revenge and aggression
- unsavoury topics
- social development: addiction, behaviour and isolation
- lack of imagination
- physical effects
- eSafety

More information about all of these topics and up-to-date lists of relevant computer games can be found at www.karen-anderson.org.

Positive Topics

There are many positives which can be taken from computer games. You might be surprised at the following list of areas where games can actually help, especially in the development of skills:

- good versus evil
- cultural awareness
- moral decision-making
- strategy, resource management and quick thinking
- consequences
- reading and maths
- perseverance
- development of dexterity, pattern awareness and hand–eye coordination
- multi-tasking and tracking simultaneous objectives
- mapping and memory
- teamwork and social/cultural awareness
- opportunity for a positive message

More information about all of these topics and up-to-date lists of relevant computer games can be found at www.karen-anderson.org.

6 A Future in Computer Games

Although you may have some pupils who just think it would be 'cool' to work with computer games, it is a hard industry to get into and the work can be difficult, laborious and pressured. However, for those pupils who are serious about becoming part of the industry it can be highly enjoyable, challenging, rewarding and would allow them to work in a field about which they are passionate.

A pupil does not have to be an ICT whizz in order to work in the games industry, although that certainly is a main skill area. Those who show talent in Art, Music or creative writing in English may also have skills needed by games studios.

This chapter discusses possible routes into the industry and the advice which you could give to pupils who are interested in working in this field. It is honest and frank. However, please be aware that there are no hard and fast rules for this and no method can be guaranteed to work better or worse than another.

You Don't Have to Study It... But It Might Help?

The message from the games industry used to be: don't study games design, enter the industry at 16 while you're still young, before you've been institutionalized, before universities have zapped your creativity; we will train you up, we will mould you…

However, things appear to have changed. Games studios have grown, teams are much larger, they work to tighter timescales and are more product-oriented – understandably as the success of the product, the game, is what keeps the studio going. It is unlikely they will have the time or resources to bring in a trainee at 16 without any skills and provide training and the time to develop technically and creatively. Although this can happen for very talented individuals who hit a lucky break, it is not a common route in.

In addition to this, colleges and universities are now providing much better games design education and giving their pupils specific, useful and relevant skills for the industry. A lot of university games departments have their own games studios, such as Canalside Studios at the University of Huddersfield, UK, who have developed games from Microsoft Xbox Live, and Digipen at the Institute of Technology, Washington USA, who created the fundamental ideas for Valve's huge hits *Portal 1* and *Portal 2*. This type of practical experience can be really attractive to games studio employers.

There are several areas of study which can lead to a career in computer games, including:

- Computer Games Design
- Multimedia
- Animation
- Programming
- Digital Art
- Music Technology

Several sixth forms and colleges are now offering Computer Games as a subject, either as part of the ICT or the Media departments. The other subjects in the list should be available for post-16 education and all are available at post-18. It would be advisable to find a practical course rather than theoretical, as to work in the industry you need to be able to show you can 'do' not just 'talk about'.

There are over 200 university courses in the UK offering game-related studies. When looking at university courses, be aware there is a difference between Games Design and Games Development. Specifically, Design courses would usually be more creative and art-based, whereas Development courses would generally involve programming and be more technical. However, the two terms are sometimes used interchangeably – always check the precise details of a course, looking at the modules to be studied. Again, look for practical courses where you can develop skills in using industry-standard software.

Experience is something which can boost your CV; but gaining it can be tricky. Games studios are sometimes reluctant to take placements as they are often working on confidential projects which they do not want their competitors to know about and also may not have time to 'look after' someone on a placement. However, occasionally there are opportunities to work at studios and it is always worth trying. Use any contacts you may have and be aware that the placement may not be paid. Also consider placements other than games studios, such as companies that develop content for mobile phones, interactive features for museums or other multimedia work. Although work experience is a good opportunity to try out the industry in which you interested in working and learning relevant skills, it also proves that you can work in a team, use communication, be professional and have other work-related skills that are involved in being an employee.

Also, do not discount any skills you learn or products you create as part of a hobby. If you like creating digital artwork, draw comic strips or mash up videos for YouTube. If they show high quality talent, then it can all count towards demonstrating that you are suited for the industry.

Importantly, you should also play games. However, it must be a wide variety of games, even ones you don't like, and you should play them with a critical eye. If you spend several hours a day getting the highest scores on the latest FPS, that does not show you have a breadth of experience of games. Try playing games from every genre, commercial and indie, classics from earlier systems – and with all of them, don't just play to win, play to experience, learn and understand what the games are about.

When looking for job opportunities in the games industry, you may wish to consider the following:

- Look directly on the games studio's website or write to them (make sure you find out the specific address and the name of a relevant person – and spell it correctly!).
- Read trade publications, such as *Edge Magazine* which contains a large section on careers in the industry.
- There are conferences and exhibitions, which are held in locations all over the world such as E3, Los Angeles USA, Game Developers Conference, San Francisco USA or the Evolve and Develop conferences, Brighton UK. It may be difficult to visit these events, but follow them online, read live blogs and twitter feeds about them, listen to podcasts summarizing them and keep your knowledge up-to-date.

Applications often consist of three core elements:

- a CV
- a portfolio
- an application form

You should always have an up-to-date CV ready as you never know when opportunity may strike! This may be in paper format or could be on a USB stick or even your own website. Application forms are likely to be specific to the employer so you cannot usually prepare these in advance.

Your portfolio should be built over time and demonstrate your very best pieces of work. If you are looking at working in a specific field, such as Games Art, your portfolio should include hand-drawn images, digital images, 3D modelling and different types of content including figures, creatures, environment, abstract, etc. In a broader portfolio you may also include mini-games which you have programmed or sample programming, animation, digital edited sound and anything else which you feel shows of your talents to the maximum. Your portfolio may be printed or it may be digital, but it should always be easily accessible, well presented and professional.

When writing to studios, applying for jobs and (hopefully) going to interviews, always remember that, although this industry is about computer games and entertainment, first and foremost it is serious about business. You should always be professional, dress smartly and represent yourself well in your behaviour.

Another aspect to remember is that the games industry has other job opportunities as well as the people who actually make the games. They need website designers, administrators, finance experts and other roles in which you may be interested.

A quick note about games testers

This can be a way to get useful experience or a start in the industry. However, being a games tester does not mean you get to sit and play games all day. You might be asked to play one particular part of a new game over and over and over again to thoroughly test it for bugs and problems and documenting what you find. It can be laborious and boring, but it would mean you were part of the games industry. There are sometimes opportunities to test games at home, occasionally with a demo released with a full game. Although this games testing is usually not paid, it can give you good experience to put on your CV – and let you see a game in development before it is released commercially.

Information About the Computer Games Industry

The games industry is a viable career opportunity for pupils. It used to be made up of very small teams, a tight-knit community and was virtually impossible to break into it. Now the teams for commercial games are getting bigger and bigger, the jobs available are broader and the companies are relatively more stable.

The types of jobs available include:

- artists
- script writers
- animators
- programmers
- audio (music/SFX)
- online technologies
- producers/directors
- testers
- marketing

The games industry in the UK is estimated to be currently worth over £4 billion and employs more than 30,000 people. In 2009, 6.7 million consoles were sold in the UK (Source: vg247. com 6/1/10) and in 2010, 63 million games (Source: eurogamer.net 4/1/11).

After the United States and Japan, the United Kingdom is the third biggest video game market, something which is not often known and demonstrates that this is a viable industry

Using Computer Games Across the Curriculum

for British pupils to aspire to enter. Some of the biggest games have been produced in the UK, such as *Grand Theft Auto* which is primarily made by Rockstar North in Scotland, Team 17 who make *Lemmings* and *Worms* are in Wakefield and the *Total War* series is developed by The Creative Assembly in Sussex.

This is an exciting time for games, a time that may not even have been foreseen by those pioneers of gaming. It is becoming the norm to have a two-console or three-console home. Games not only have stories, but also back stories, sequels and prequels. Some games are even delivered free across the Internet (such as *MapleStory* – a huge online game which is completely free). The lines between media are becoming blurred: for each movie release there is often an accompanying computer game. TV shows like *Lost* and BBC's *Sherlock* have websites which give extra experiences to fans, not just information about the shows, but games, puzzles and interaction with the characters.

For pupils who are interested in working in the games industry, the advice I give in general is: it is hard to get in; they are looking only for people with true talent; however, if you are good enough, want it enough and work hard enough, it is a hugely exciting and rewarding field in which to work. I would always encourage pupils to research more into it, consider a specific area where they might specialize and ask themselves why they want to become part of the games industry. If it is because they like playing games and would think it was 'cool', I might start gently dissuading them. However if they said they had a passion for games, felt they had the right skills (even if they needed developing) and wanted to be part of a team creating entertainment for the public, (or words to that effect) I would certainly encourage them to explore it further.

Glossary

age classification Games in the UK are classified by PEGI (Pan-European Game Information). This is done by age: 3, 7, 12, 16 and 18. It also indicates content including violence, bad language, sex or gambling. Badges for age and content should be shown on games sold in the UK.

casual games There are generally two types of game: casual and serious. Casual games are designed to be played for a short time, do not require commitment from the player and are generally simple to understand. Examples include *Minesweeper*, *Tetris* and *Angry Birds*.

cloud gaming services (Steam and OnLive) Simply put, cloud computing uses internet-based hardware, rather than hardware by the user. For example, files might be stored 'in the cloud' rather than on the user's computer. Cloud gaming services provide games from the cloud, rather than the player having to buy a disk.

commercial label Some games are published on a commercial label, which means they are backed by a large game publishing company which will give support in terms of producing disks, advertising and other areas. For the opposite, see indie games.

console A console is a piece of computer hardware on which games can be played such as Xbox 360, PlayStation 3 or Nintendo Wii.

console networks (Xbox Live and PlayStation Network) A console network is where different players can connect and play with other players around the world. Microsoft uses Xbox Live, Sony uses PlayStation Network and Nintendo use Wii Online.

controller A controller is the device held in the player's hand which controls the game. Xbox 360 and PlayStation 3 use traditional game controllers, whereas Wii uses the Wii Remote (which is motion controlled). Also Xbox 360 has an extra controller called Kinect which is also motion controlled but the player does not need to hold anything in their hands.

co-operatively (co-op) Co-op allows players to play multiplayer but together, on the same team. They need to work to help each other to play the game.

cut scenes Cut scenes are the animated sequences at the beginning and throughout the game. Generally they are not interactive, advance the story and often used to load the next sequence of the game.

environment The environment is the world in which the game is played.

first-person shooter (FPS) An FPS game is one where the player sees through the eyes of the main character and usually involves shooting with a variety of weapons. Examples include *Call of Duty*, *Halo* and *Half Life*.

free roaming Free roaming means that the player can go wherever they want in the game world (environment), as opposed to other games which can be linear, forcing the player to take a certain route.

genre Genre is the category in which a game can be placed. This may be based on the type of game play or content.

glasses-less 3D 3D technology has been around for decades, but always with glasses, from the red and blue lenses from the 80s to 3D films at the cinema. Glasses-less 3D uses a 3D screen which does not need glasses, as used in the 3DS.

handheld/portable gaming Games consoles are static and have to be played in one place, whereas handheld game devices can be carried and moved around. This started with devices such as GameBoy and now uses Nintendo DS/3DS, PlayStation Portable/Vita and even smartphones such as the iPhone.

hardware Hardware is the physical equipment such as a console or controller.

HUD (heads up display) A HUD is the graphics displayed on screen which are static while the player plays the game. This might include health, experience, a map and other information to help the player.

realistic physics Games might use realistic physics which mimic the real world. This would include gravity and momentum.

Independent games (indies) Indies are games which are not published by commercial labels but are often self-published on the internet. They are generally developed by one person, two people or a very small team, and can be given away for free, distributed freely but accepting donations or for a small charge.

intellectual property (IP) Intellectual property are ideas, designs, characters and other non-physical property.

interactive fiction (IF) Interactive fiction is a type of game which is text-based. The players type in commands and the game produces on-screen text to further the story. The most famous game of this type is *Zork*.

internet-enabled computer A computer which can be connected to the internet.

Local Area Network (LAN) A LAN is a small network where devices are connected together in a small geographical area. For gaming, a group of PCs could be joined together in the same room.

machinima Machinima is a movie which uses game footage instead of video footage or original animation.

mini-games Mini-games are small games – see casual games.

MMOs (Massively Multiplayer Online) Massively Multiplayer Online games are ones which you can play with large groups of people all over the world, usually in huge game worlds. Examples of this include *World of Warcraft* and *Lord of the Rings Online*.

multiplayer Multiplayer means being able to play with other players. That might be players in the same room, on the same console, or it could be with players anywhere in the world using the internet.

multi-touch pads Multi-touch pads allow a user to use more than one finger on a screen such as to pinch zoom like on an iPhone or iPad.

NPCs (non-playing characters) NPCs are characters in a game which is controlled by the computer, rather than a live player.

peripherals Peripherals are devices which are connected to a computer or a console.

pickups Pickups are objects within a game which a character can pick up e.g., a heart to increase health.

pixelated A pixelated picture is one which has become blocky. This can happen in low-quality pictures, when they are enlarged too far.

platform A platform is the technology used to play a game. A game may be made for only one platform, or for a range of platforms.

platformer A platformer game is where the character must jump between different platforms and the game is often 2D and side-scrolling, such as classic Mario games.

point-and-click adventure Point-and-click adventure games allow the player to use a device (such as a mouse on a PC or stylus on a Nintendo DS) and click on parts of the screen to move the character or select objects. Very often the games involve puzzles and interesting storylines.

polygons Polygons are the shapes which are used to create graphics in games. The more polygons used, the more realistic the graphics. Voxels are also sometimes used instead of polygons.

processor, RAM and graphics card The processor is the brains of a computer, measured by speed, such as GHz (gigahertz).
RAM (random access memory) is temporary memory which allows the computer to access data faster. It is measured in size, such as Gb (gigabytes).
A graphics card is the part of a computer which is used to run the graphics.

protagonist/antagonist A protagonist is the main character in a story, usually a 'goodie'. An antagonist is the main enemy of the protagonist, as the 'baddie'.

role-playing game (RPG) A role-playing game asks the player to take on a role and play this throughout the game. Often these games are fantasy-based.

server A server is a central computer which controls other computers or consoles.

seventh generation consoles Seventh generation consoles include Xbox 360, PlayStation 360 and Nintendo Wii.

simulators Simulators are programs which imitate real-world situations; for example, in flight simulators the player might be responsible for a plane which is as realistic to the real life-situation of flying a plane as possible.

sixth generation consoles Sixth generation consoles include original Xbox, PlayStation 2, Nintendo GameCube and Sony Dreamcast.

strategy game A strategy game is one where the player must use tactics and skill to win the game. Examples of strategy games include the *Civilisation* series, *Age of Empires* and *Worms*

strategy guide book A strategy guide is a book which explains how the game works, how to complete it and provides extra information about the detail of the game.

system link System link is where more than one console is connected together so more players can take part in multiplayer. For example, an Xbox 360 can take four controllers, but two connected together with system link can take eight.

system requirements Systems requirements are the minimum technical requirements needed in order to play a game. Often games will give a minimum requirement and a preferred requirement.

tablets and smartphones A table is a handheld, portable device such as an iPad. A smartphone is a mobile phone which gives more functionality than just making calls and sending texts, such as iPhones and Android and Windows mobiles.

tetrominoes Tetrominoes are the seven shapes which can be used in the game of *Tetris*.

top-down strategy See strategy game.

tournament structure A tournament structure is where each person plays another player and the winner of each pairing then goes onto the next round. The winners then pair up and play each other. This pattern keeps going until a final with two players, and the one who wins becomes the ultimate winner of the tournament.

VLE A VLE (virtual learning environment) is a computer system which tools for teachers such as communicating with pupils, setting interactive work, collecting digital submissions of work and tracking assessments.

walkthroughs A walkthrough is the instructions for a player to complete a game. Also see strategy guide book.

wrist straps Wrist straps are provided with Wii Remotes and should always be worn when used to prevent the remote flying out of the player's hand.

Xbox Live Arcade See console networks.

Subject Matrix

Most activities, although generally particular to one subject, may fit into another. If you are looking for activities for a subject, please use the subject matrix below to direct you to activities which can be used in that subject.

English and literacy

Maths and numeracy

Science

Languages

History

Geography

Art and design

Music

Technology subjects

Physical education

Religious studies

Drama

Business studies

Media and film studies

Skills Matrix

Please use the subject matrix below to direct you to activities which can be used to develop and use specific skills.

Writing skills

Numeracy

Teamwork

Creativity and imagination

Motor skills and movement

Problem solving, strategy and planning

Typing skills

Art skills

Debating and discussing

Researching

Index of Games

Game	Studio	Publisher	Year	Platform(s)	Pages
Fable series	Big Blue Box	Microsoft Game Studios	2004	Xbox	33, 34, 47
	Lionhead Studios		2008/2010	Xbox 360	
		Feral Interactive	2008/2011	Microsoft Windows	
	Robosoft Technologies		2004	Mac OS X	
Final Fantasy	Square	Square	1987	Nintendo Entertainment System	27
				PlayStation	
				Game Boy Advance	
				Mobile phones	
				PlayStation Portable	
				Virtual Console	
				PlayStation Network	
				iOS	
				Windows Phone	
Flower	Thatgamecompany	Sony Computer Game Entertainment	2009	PlayStation 3	27
Football Manager Series	Sports Interactive	Sega	2009/2011	PlayStation Portable	30
			2010/2011/2012	iOS	
				Microsoft Windows	
			2010/2011		
Game Dev Story	Kairosoft		2010	iOS	29
				Android	
Halo series	Bungie Software	Microsoft Game Studios	2001/2004/2009/2010/2011/2012	Xbox	33, 34, 52, 62, 74, 76
	Destineer Studios	Destineer Studios	2003/2005/2007	Microsoft Windows	
			2006	Mac OS X	
Ico	Team Ico	Sony Computer Game Entertainment	2001	PlayStation 2	27
			2011	PlayStation 3	

Game	Studio	Publisher	Year	Platform(s)	Pages
Ilo Milo	SouthEnd Interactive Microsoft Game Studio	Microsoft Game Studio	2010 2010	Xbox Live Arcade Windows Phone 7	25, 62
Limbo	Playdead	Microsoft Game Studio Playdead	2010	Xbox Live Arcade PlayStation 3 Network Microsoft Windows Mac OS X Linux	16, 25, 35
Little Big Planet	Media Molecule SCE Cambridge Studio	Sony Computer Entertainment Europe	2008	PlayStation 3 PlayStation Portable PlayStation Vita	25, 74, 78
Machinarium	Amanita Design	Amanita Design	2009	Microsoft Windows OS X Linux PlayStation 3 (PSN) iPad 2 BlackBerry PlayBook Android	27, 34
Mass Effect	BioWare Demiurge studios BioWare	Microsoft Game Studio Electronic Arts Electronic Arts	2007 2008 2010/2012 2012	Xbox 360 Microsoft Windows Microsoft Windows Xbox 360 PlayStation 3 Wii U	32, 33, 34, 39, 55
Metal Gear Solid 4: Guns of the Patriots	Kojima Productions	Konami	2008	PlayStation 3	32, 33
Minecraft	Mojang 4J Studios	Mojang	2011 2012	Java Platform Java Applet Android iOS Xbox 360	16, 26, 63

Game	Studio	Publisher	Year	Platform(s)	Pages
Okami	Clover Studio	Capcom	2006	PlayStation 2	27
			2008	Wii	
Rollercoaster Tycoon Series	Chris Sawyer Productions	Infogrames	2002	Microsoft Windows	30
				Microsoft Windows	
	Frontier Developments	Atari Inc	2004	Mac OS X	
The Secret of Monkey Island Special Edition	Lucasfilm Games	LucasArts	2009	iOS	32, 33, 65
				Mac OS X	
				Micrsoft Windows	
				PlayStation Network	
				Xbox Live	
Wet	Artificial Mind and Movement	Bethesda Softworks	2009	Xbox 360 PlayStation 3	25
XIII	Ubisoft Paris	Ubisoft	2003	Microsoft Windows	25
				PlayStation 2	
				Xbox Original	
	Southend Interactive			Nintendo GameCube	
				Mobile Phone	
		Feral Interactive		Mac OS X	

Index